THE ALL NEW
OFFICIAL COMPANION

Darren Crosdale

**Based on the hit television series
created by Kevin Williamson**

TED SMART

Dedication

Mommy, this book I dedicate to you as the mere fact it exists is down to you. Thank you.

Acknowledgements

Thanks to –
The crew of *Dawson's Creek*, Helen for the walks, the talks, the acupuncture; Darnel for the giggles, the hamster and the honesty; Errol for the technical assistance – I taught you well; Derek – the only other writer who could understand the block and help to shift it; Cindy Irwin; Jake Lingwood – thanks for trusting me to work the magic again and Natalie Jerome – good luck and I await your story.
Everyone at Wanstead High School, Ebury Press, and Columbia TriStar Television.

This edition produced for The Book People Ltd, Hall Wood Avenue, Haydock, St Helens WA11 5AU

First published in UK in 2001 by
Ebury Press
Random House, 20 Vauxhall Bridge Road, London SW1V 2SA

Random House Australia (Pty) Limited
20 Alfred Street, Milsons Point, Sydney, New South Wales 2061, Australia

Random House New Zealand Limited
18 Poland Road, Glenfield, Auckland 10, New Zealand

Random House South Africa (Pty) Limited
Endulini, 5A Jubilee Road, Parktown 2193, South Africa

Random House UK Limited Reg. No. 954009

A CIP catalogue record for this book is available from the British Library

Design by Dan Newman/Perfect Bound Ltd

Front cover photo by Art Streiber
Interior photos by Art Streiber, Fred Norris, Guy D'Alema and Marc Kayne

Printed and bound in Great Britain by Biddles of Guildford

Papers used by Ebury Press are natural, recyclable products made from wood grown in sustainable forests.

Contents

Introduction

By Paul Stupin, Executive Producer

I remember the first day of shooting like it was yesterday. It was a beautiful day in early April, 1997. We had just cast James Van Der Beek a week before and had received the official green light immediately thereafter. There we all were, at some nightmarishly early hour of the morning, gathered behind the house that would become Dawson's home in Wilmington, North Carolina. Joshua Jackson had flown all night and went right from the airport into a monster suit (a wardrobe for the first scene up). One of Katie Holmes' sisters, who had accompanied her to the shoot, was painting a watercolor of the creek. There was a real sense of passion, energy and excitement in the air. I felt like we were on to something really special that day, something unique and lasting.

Now, several seasons later – and maybe I'm coming off like a proud father – I can say that I was right. So much has happened to our characters in four seasons. They have all matured in ways even I didn't know they would.

Dawson has really grown into a man these past few years. Gone is the wide-eyed romantic with dreams of making it big in Hollywood. In his place is a confident young man with renewed belief in himself. This past year he endured the death of a dear friend, the loss and re-emergence of a friendship with his soulmate and the ordeal of getting over the betrayal of a best friend. He fell in love with someone other than Joey and realized that to be truly happy, he must move forward and not backward. Dawson may have matured the most out of all of our characters over these four years.

And then there's Joey. This past year she experienced a deep love with someone other than her soulmate. Who ever thought it could happen? Joey Potter falling in love with Pacey Witter? But she did, and it was more than puppy love. Though Joey's love for Dawson will always be, she shared an adult relationship with Pacey that took them both to another level. For most of her high-school life, Joey Potter was looking for something – and that something was who she was outside of Dawson, outside of Capeside. This year she finally found out. She is the woman who got into her college of choice, who will make it out of Capeside, and who can love deeply while learning to love herself.

Then there's the man Joey chose to love deeply – Pacey. He has come full circle from the lovable loser, to the hero, to the boy hell-bent on self-destruction. For a while, Pacey really went through the ringer. His first real girlfriend, Andie, was unfaithful… he barely made it to the 12th grade… and his best buddy since childhood disowned him when he found out about his relationship with Joey. But this year Pacey fell head over heels for someone he never imagined could love him back, and realized what real love is. He grew closer to his sister and brother, and rebuilt his relationship with Dawson. If there's one thing Pacey is, he's a survivor. He has grown out of the goofy sidekick into a dashing leading man of his own.

But if there's anyone who knows about being a survivor, it's Jen. She has re-emerged from rock bottom to spread her wings in so many different ways. She became strong enough to reject her past weaknesses and temptations in the form of Drue Valentine. She found it in herself this year to face her demons, and return to New York for the first time. She wasn't always strong enough to face her past – or her present sometimes – but with the love and support she found in Capeside, and some therapy, Jen managed to confront her father and forgive herself for things she couldn't control. She found unconditional love with Grams and Jack and, with their help, made it to college.

Jack is the character, for me, that really breaks the mold. He's everything to everyone, without missing a beat. His journey was a harder one, but this past year he really matured into a strong young man. He found it within himself this year to be proud of himself and his sexuality. He found a surrogate family when his own wasn't always close at hand. He reconciled himself with his father but saw his sister leave. And, hardest of all, he finally let himself get close to someone and have a meaningful relationship.

And then there's his sister, Andie – the spunky, brainy, yet beautifully fragile girl. She finally came to terms with the fact that she doesn't always have to be perfect. She let herself take it easy for once and took off a semester to spend abroad. Though she missed her brother terribly, she felt it okay to leave knowing she would see him again soon and that his surrogate sister Jen would always be there for him. Andie finally let go of Pacey, however difficult, and accepted his relationship with Joey.

As for new characters, one of my favorites in a long time has to be Drue Valentine, the ever-present bad boy. He strolled into town and rattled everyone's cages, especially that of his old friend and sometime paramour, Jen Lindley. Drue is the gum on the bottom of your shoe that you can't quite scrape off, though underneath all that bravado, once in a rare while, you might see some real feelings and complexities.

And lastly there's Gretchen Witter. No-nonsense, tough on the outside but with a heart as big as the ocean. She waltzed into town and turned things a little inside out when she fell in love with Dawson. She helped her younger brother Pacey through some pretty tough times while bravely facing her own.

So, you remember that excitement and passion I talked about that first day of shooting? Well, it's never gone away. In spite of hurricanes, sudden snowstorms and unforeseen production problems, it's stronger than ever.

As I think back to where all our characters have been, I get equally excited about where they're going. I care deeply about these characters and love seeing their stories unfold. Dawson, Joey, Pacey, Jen, Jack, Andie, and everyone in between, have a special place in my heart. I hope they do in yours as well.

Setting the Scene

Wow. Four seasons. That is a lot of conversations, introspection, love, infatuation, tears, regrets, adulations, break-ups, and make-ups. But most importantly, it has been four seasons about the altering nature of friendships. The first-ever episode, which opened with the subtext-heavy conversation of a teenage boy and girl discussing the difficulty of platonic relationships, has grown far beyond anyone's dreams. It has grown into a show that is deemed worthy, yet has lost none of the wit and charm that made it feisty and popular in the first place.

Dawson's Creek is a show that survives by focusing on the timeless narratives of love, friendships, and family. The topics its articulate teens have taken in their stride – adoption, drugs, teen sex, homosexuality, mental illness, divorce, ambition – may sound like the depressing litany of a modern television talk show. But held together by a gang who are more concerned with integrity and their pals, it has never taken on the persona of an issues-led show.

After its fourth super-successful season, Dawson's Creek has proved that a television show could deal with challenging issues without being salacious or depressing. Its characters are articulate enough to express their loves, hates, fears, and ambitions, and remain realistic. Sure, they can deconstruct a kiss to death, but that's the thing with Dawson Leery, Joey Potter, Pacey Witter, Jen Lindley, Jack and Andie McPhee – they often talk themselves into circles we in the outside world delight in deconstructing.

Self-referential and deliciously irreverent, the end of the first season of Dawson's Creek, Episode #112, Decisions, sees Joey deconstructing the conventions of television drama cliff-hangers: "The producers put their characters in some contrived situation to make the audience think something will change, but it never does." Was she correct in her assessment? Perhaps, but Dawson's Creek broke the boundaries of most teen shows in its first season.

Incidentally, the first season was only 13 episodes because hey, no-one actually knew if this little programme about kids and their drama would take off! And this delicious awareness of itself as a show in the real world is

deliberately referred to time and time again, just in case anyone gets a little too caught up in the melodrama. It is a show for the media-savvy. Just ask Jen Lindley. In Episode #323, *True Love*, she says: "We're not in Capeside at all, Toto. But some alternate reality where our intellects are sharper, our quips wittier, and our hearts repeatedly broken while, faintly, in the distance, some soon-to-be-dated contempo pop music plays."

Then there's Pacey's take on the melodrama of life. In the opening for Season IV, Episode #401, *Coming Home*, he says to Joey, thinking about not returning to Capeside after three months at sea: "And just what would we be missing from the Land of Poorly Scripted Melodrama? Hmm? Another year's worth of recycled plotlines and tiresome self-realizations."

We've had teenage drama before. We've had really good teenage drama before. Good teen drama resonates with viewers on a personal level and helps them achieve further understanding of situations they may have been through, or situations they will soon go through. We've had two seasons of *Dawson's Creek*. But like the characters the show has created for us to love, it has grown and matured. *Dawson's Creek* makes you love it that little bit more, makes you laugh that little bit more, perhaps makes you cry that little bit more.

Dawson has matured. The introspective, smart teen has faced challenges from which the younger Dawson would have been hard-pressed to emerge. His deepest held notions, his love of film, his life-long friendships, and his parents' relationship have been challenged and thrown him into a turmoil he had to work hard to extract himself from. Back in Season I, one of Dawson's most pressing trials was building up the courage to ask Jen Lindley, the new girl in town, out on a date to the school prom. In Season IV, Dawson has to cope with the terrible burden of seeing his soulmate Joey fall for his best friend Pacey. It hardly compares. In Season II, Dawson was on the verge of taking advice from Capeside's version of Satan – Abby Morgan – about what to do if his parents divorced. In Season III, Dawson had to cope with seeing them get back together and delightfully wreck his only-child status. The Leery lad had some pressing trials. He may not have held his head high as he battled through them, he may not have struck upon the correct course of action the very first time, but he did manage, at the end, to allow his preternatural instinct to do good to surface.

Joey has matured. She was always the hard-working cookie of the bunch but because her nose was always down in her books, she rarely took time out to realize that the wonder years were slipping by. In Season I, Joey struggled hard to suppress her feelings for her best friend, Dawson. In Season III, because of

Joey to Pacey: "We talk like we know what's going on, but we don't. We don't know anything. We're really young and we're gonna screw up a lot. We're gonna keep changing our minds and even sometimes our hearts. And through all that, the only real thing we can offer each other is forgiveness."

her debt of friendship to Dawson, she felt the need to suppress her feelings for Pacey. But Pacey made her realize that, for once, she deserved to follow her heart. His energy and fun took her to places she had never been before, both literally and figuratively. She achieved happiness, fleeting though it was. A letter, written long ago by Joey's mother Lillian, helped her understand how proud everyone was of her. She had achieved her dream of getting into college, and a friend's assistance proved that true friendship will endure.

Pacey has matured. The group comedian, ever ready with a wisecrack, has struggled with school. It is a place where he would have shone were it not for the rules and the detentions and the distractions. Despite Pacey's incapacity to deal with standardized testing, he has proved time and time again that he fully understands what friendship and love are about. His break up with Andie came as a blow but then again, so did his feelings for Joey. He fought those feelings for Joey because of his friend Dawson. But in the end, he ultimately made the correct decision in following where his heart led him.

Jen too has matured. The founder-member of the Bitter Club at last eased up on herself long enough to fall truly, madly, deeply in love. The relationship with Henry Parker posed its own problems. Her relationships with the others also came into question when she allowed herself to be led astray by past indiscretions on the prowl from New York. Hopefully, though, Jen has permanently banished the demons that have haunted her for years by seeking

professional help. Jen's relationships with Jack and Grams foundered but were restored and bolstered by everyone admitting how much they needed each other and how true friends are always willing to make sacrifices.

Jack has also grown up in a number of ways. He has become more comfortable with his sexuality but also refused to be defined solely by it. He is also a footballer, a friend, a brother. His father worked hard to rekindle a relationship with his only son and through the advice of friends, Jack learned to forgive and move on. He has battled discrimination and emerged with his dignity intact. His broad shoulders have helped both his sister Andie and his best friend Jen in their times of need.

And so to Andie. The highly-strung genius overcame her mental illness only to return to Capeside and lose her boyfriend, Pacey, through her infidelity. She regained her composure, however, by keeping busy and even managed to win Pacey's friendship again. She made a serious mistake in cheating in the practice SAT test but her honesty shone through in the end. The fact that she achieved her childhood dream where college was concerned showed she never needed any cheat sheet anyway. After her near-fatal trial with drugs, Andie went to Italy for a breather. But before she did that, she proved herself to be an organized, selfless and super-smart friend by helping the others restore something which they had lost; true friendship.

Although *Dawson's Creek* focuses on the lives of these six teenagers, the people on the periphery of the show have also matured in their own way. Mitch and Gale Leery, Grams, Bessie, and Mr McPhee all prove that no matter how old you get, you can still learn new tricks. They have had to deal with a variety of changes in their own lives and accept the teens they love are moving ever onward and upward.

This Guide not only delights in Seasons III and IV but also references Seasons I and II. We observe how characters have matured and, in media terms, explore how *Dawson's Creek* has become a worldwide venture. There are in-depth character analyses as well as quirky looks at aspects of their lives, loves, and passions. There is a section on the impact of *Dawson's Creek* on the Internet. We explore how the show has created an online presence that continues to lead the way in interactive entertainment as well as provide a plethora of material the television show does not have time to access. As always, there are interviews with the creators of the show. We find out how storylines are carefully delineated, with the primary focus remaining character truth, and high standards of production.

Watching Seasons III and IV has been like watching a scene on a nature program that has been speeded up; you know, the seed germinating and growing into a sapling. We look at Dawson, Joey, Pacey, Jen, Jack, and Andie and ponder: when did they get so smart, so witty, so capable of making mistakes, picking themselves up, and carrying on? And that is the pleasure to be derived from tracing the Creek back to its source.

Dawson's Creek Episode Guide

SEASON III
Like A Virgin .... Episode #301
Written by Tammy Ader
Directed by Greg Prange

As ever, the movie Dawson is watching gives a hint of what is to come.

Returning to Capeside on a bus and watching the Tom Cruise movie *Risky Business*, Dawson falls asleep only to wake to a vision that is every high-school boy's dream. She must have sat opposite him while he slumbered. The Girl starts conversing and it's only Dawson's intelligent movie chat that saves him from crashing and burning. But once he starts relating the trauma surrounding Joey, it's The Girl's turn to fall asleep.

Joey is having trouble with her octopus-like colleague Rob Logan, at the gas station where she is now working. Senator Logan's eldest son is only working there as a punishment.

Jack and Jen are like a married couple in Grams' house, so well do they get on. At school, Belinda McGovern and the rest of the cheerleaders irk Jen and Jack. Ironic as ever, Jen pretends to try out for cheerleading squad but instead humiliates Belinda with a wicked diatribe – winning herself the top position!

Girl:
"You're a virgin aren't you?"
Dawson:
"What comes before virgin?"

Dawson regales Pacey with the narrative of The Girl, whose name he never caught. Pacey's interested but more keen to get his best buddy on talking terms with Joey. Dawson reckons it's over and he's now in the mood to break free of his old mold. But the bravado's a front, as the sight of Joey equals hyperventilation. Pacey "saves" him by whisking him to a stripclub declaring this is the year Dawson gets "laid". The waitress is none other than The Girl and Pacey (mis)advises Dawson to impress her with a whizz in Mitch's boat. The Girl gets frisky, and Dawson crashes into the pier where Joey's working. She's concerned for Dawson – until she sees that he is all right and accompanied by The Girl – also known as Eve. "And suddenly everything becomes clear."

The $3,000 damage equals doom for Dawson – until Pacey's cunning plan for Eve to invite some stripper friends equals a fund-raising party. The rockin'

and rollin' party becomes too much for Dawson, who retires to his room – only to be met by Joey. She apologizes for dumping him following her father's arrest and makes a move on him. "It's not the same anymore, Joey," he says. She's scathing in her rage. "It's not my fault if you're still a virgin." He does not rise to her anger and instead confides he still loves her.

Downstairs, Eve looks at Dawson with celebration twinkling in her eye. Pacey whispers in his ear, it's Joey or Eve – the Madonna or the Jezebel. Dawson requests that his best friend look after his ex-girlfriend. "Just watch out for her for a few days." Leery's about to go with Eve when Mitch returns from a business trip. Dawson chooses responsibility over delicious recklessness.

Pacey's first friendly overtures towards Joey are met with cat-like anger until he reminds her that he knows what it's like to have to let go of someone you love.

Episode Music

Bob Seger – 'Old Time Rock & Roll'
Pretenders – 'Who's Who'
Garbage – 'Sleep Together'
Buckcherry – 'Dead Again'
Tricky Woo – 'Let Us Sing'
Garbage – 'Push It'
Mary Beth – 'Hold On'

Homecoming . . . . Episode #302
Written by Greg Berlanti
Directed by Melanie Mayron

Making out at the movies takes on a whole new dimension.

Dawson's honesty pleased Pacey and he and Joey are getting on as friends. That's not a descriptor to apply to Eve – who turns up at school as a senior – as she offers him "scorching hot, unbridled, mind-altering sex" even though Dawson confesses to not being over Joey. Roped into filming

a sequence for the upcoming pep rally (the opening to the school football season) Principal Green and Mitch (Capeside High's new football coach) tell Dawson he has to create some propaganda by portraying the Minutemen as winners, when in fact they're long-time losers.

Andie:

"Jen's a cheerleader and Jack's on the football team? I got sane and everybody else went crazy."

While persuading Jen to treat cheerleading as an opportunity to make her unique mark on the school, Jack inadvertently impresses Coach Mitch with his football skills. Together with a lad called Henry, they work pigskin magic and Mitch wants Jack on the team. A taken-aback McPhee would rather not be: "... the gay kid on the football team..." fearing ridicule but Mitch spells out the fact that they could both do with a win in their lives at this moment in time.

Dawson's auditorium show for the pep rally is packed. Henry and Jen exchange a glance that suggests love is in the air. And indeed it is, for as Dawson's film rolls, Eve pounces on her prey. Let's hope Dawson's not a Minuteman. They're behind the flickering screen, which raises to reveal them, clothes awry, to a clapping crowd. Dawson, for once, laps up the attention – until he spots Joey's oh-so-hurt face.

Mr McPhee had at first not wanted Jack home. "You can't deal with having a gay son and having me around would mean doing just that," Jack spits. But now he's on the football team, Mr McPhee would not mind him coming home to roost. Jack declines, though he does not rule out moving in a little later on.

Andie's ebullient at the sight of Pacey when he arrives to pick her up from the hospital but her "friend" Marc has him worried. Back in Capeside, all Pacey's attempts to spend quality time with Andie are rebuffed, and she finally admits she slept with Marc. Pacey is undoubtedly devastated and storms off leaving Andie likewise. Joey counsels Pacey wisely: "We're really young and we're gonna screw up a lot." She says it's inadvisable to lose oneself to anger. Returning to Andie, he breaks up with her, feeling as if his love "wasn't strong enough in the first place."

Episode Music

Moby – 'Body Rock'
The Nines – 'Days & Days'
Tuck & Patti – 'Time After Time'

Dawson apologizes to Joey who says Eve helped her realize that they have to move on. They have gone from friends, to a couple, to friends, to a couple, and decide that now they are simply, Dawson and Joey.

None of the Above .... Episode #303
Written by Bonnie Schneider & Hadley Davis
Directed by Patrick Norris

It was Eve, after all, who first ate from the apple of knowledge.

The upcoming practice SAT exams have our gang responding in their various characteristic ways. While Dawson revises, Eve lounges on his bed. She likens herself to a temptress whose role it is to test the hero's moral fibre. Joey's stressed as she is aiming to win a scholarship. A-student Andie's completely in tune, cramming like a lawyer. Jen surprises Jack with her intelligence while Pacey – sleeps!

Joey seeks Dawson's help for relaxation — but he's got Eve plans and Joey's not one to play gooseberry. Nonchalantly, Eve hands Dawson an advance copy of the test. That apple is tempting indeed — not so much for Dawson but for his pals. In the library, they weigh pros and cons. The McPhees want it left unopened, while Pacey's desperate to rip it open. Jen's dying for a peek while Joey wants no part of it until the word scholarship is mentioned. Saved (or unsaved) by a fire drill bell, when they return, the test paper is gone!

Eve shifts Dawson's habit of trust and he starts questioning his friends, ending with an ultimatum to return the test to his locker at the end of the day. The bare locker assaults Dawson's morals but Eve's unsurprised: "Welcome to the real world, Dawson, where the first person to stab you in the back is your best friend."

Andie takes Pacey aside and returns all the gifts and photos he had ever given her. Ouch. He later goes to Joey, drunk, for counsel. She's a good friend. Enter Real World Dawson throwing accusatory glances at Pacey who, though drunk, ends up calling him a "self-righteous bastard". Dawson tells Pacey he's a "smug, cold-hearted, son of a bitch" for treating Andie the way he has. They end up punching, Joey ends up shouting at Dawson, and he ends up sighing gravely and departing. Joey tends to Pacey, warning him not to take Dawson's words (or blows!) to heart. Later, Eve finds Dawson sitting on the dock of his bay, contemplating "that stupid test". She's calm in her attempt to make him understand her darker view of the world.

Mitch drills Jack in football, failing to heed his lament that the others are picking on him because of his sexuality. As well as bandages, Jen doles out "don't

Dawson to Eve (about teen show *Felicity*): "If you've seen one hour of overanalytical teen angst, haven't you seen 'em all?"

give up" advice. Henry helps Jack get his game together and reveals his feelings for Jen. Jack reckons his chances are slim due to the age difference. Jack is transformed into a powerhouse player who receives team respect.

Episode Music

Nine Days – 'Absolutely'
Train – 'Swaying'
Chris Isaak – 'Speak of the Devil'
Sue Medley – 'You Won't See Me Cry'
Evan & Jaron – 'From Heart to Heart'

The real SAT test is introduced by the indomitable Principal Green. Our gang of six are in their various guises: Andie, prepared; Pacey, swollen-lipped; Joey, cheering him up. Dawson, watching the exchange, realizes he's been pushed to the periphery and walks out of the test. Outside, he's joined by Pacey – they're friends again. The test thief? Andie, who fills in her answer sheet by memory.

Home Movies .... Episode #304
Written by Jeffrey Stepakoff
Directed by Nick Marck

Any given football day you will find emotions flare.

Pacey helps Dawson prepare for a documentary on Capeside High's upcoming big football game. Old footage reveals the wonder years of a little Dawson meeting a little Joey for the first time. Dawson's documentary focuses on Jack, who is as comfortable answering questions on his sexuality as he is on football. Mitch however, declines to give an interview and then reveals that he would rather Dawson didn't make the film, even though there's a chance it will be shown on the local network.

Joey to Dawson
(on seeing him at Logan's Marina): "You must be lost – Bimbo Cove is just up the creek. Right past Brainless Bay."

Pacey encourages Joey to cut class to show her something. Unfortunately, they get nabbed by Principal Green. The glint in his eye equals a cruel and unusual punishment. The Minutemen Mule, the school mascot, will this year be

comprised of Ms Potter and Mr Witter. The choice between ass-end or head-end is theirs to make.

Henry Parker, completely smitten with Jen, cannot even focus his gaze on her lithe form clearly. Jen notices Henry as she's protesting against cheerleading as "nothing but a sexist attempt to objectify the female body". The other cheerleaders emulate her Doc Martens and fishnets dress sense and inform her of the after-game auction for a kiss with the cheerleader captain. That's where Jen draws the line. Her "polyester molest-me skirt" is itching enough without further humiliation. She quits. Grams helps to convince her otherwise as the proceeds of the kiss go to the local orphanage.

The next day, Dawson requests Joey's advice about the documentary. Dawson reminds Joey that his dad has had it rough in recent years and the road is only now less bumpy. Joey warns him that if he makes the film, Mitch's self-respect would be piqued, but Dawson would not be true to himself. Dawson leaves, giving her a copy of the *Boy meets Girl* tape, which shows the first time Dawson ever met Joey..

Andie's a bundle of nerves after bumping into someone from Educational Testing Services. Thus, when Green requests a meeting, she's terrified. Transpires he wants her to chair a student disciplinary board.

On top of that, she's doubtful the documentary will smooth McPhee father/son relations. When Jack next sees Dawson, he expresses his doubt but Dawson reminds Jack of his original aim to make someone like him "less afraid." Dawson's segment airs, but he gets no fatherly approval. Their row has Dawson holler how tired he is being the mature Leery: "Giving you advice. Walking in on you having sex! I'm the kid around here."

During the football match, Jack cannot fly as the opponents are constantly infringing him. Dawson's cunning plan mends father/son rift and enables the Minutemen to break the habit of losing. Time for the auctioned kiss and Jen's stunned to discover Henry's paid $500 for the privilege. Jen's also voted Homecoming Queen, which goes against everything she stands for.

And just what was the big surprise Pacey led Joey astray for? A boat, Pacey's very own water vehicle that he's going to name *True Love*.

Episode Music

Bleach – 'Static'
Sue Medley – 'Break the Chain'
Jude – 'I'm Sorry Now'
Mad Lion – 'Go To War'
Atomic Fireballs – 'Man With A Hex'
Jude – 'I Do'

Indian Summer .... Episode #305
Written by Gina Fattore & Tom Kapinos
Directed by Lou Antonio

Just a question, but what did really happen to Movie Night?

Mid heat-wave, the lads note Movie Night lacks females: "Didn't we once upon a time have a couple of really cute girlfriends?" Film noir offers a metaphor for Eve – who Dawson spies prowling at Grams'. His attempt to wrest the truth from her makes Eve threaten him with the stolen practice SAT test.

Next day, Dawson searches high and low for Eve. She's not even registered at the school where she claimed to be a senior. Doug advises Dawson to

Jen to Jack
**(on Henry worshipping her):
"He's a teenage boy – he'll
worship anything in a
Wonderbra."**

look for her at the laundromat. Pacey keeps Dawson company on the stakeout, and offers the pearl of wisdom that certain women enter a young man's life to fulfil a role, Tamara Jacobs – the teacher Pacey had an affair with – being a prime example. When Eve shows, they trail her to an old boat. After Eve's departure, Dawson breaks in and manages to lift a picture, before being lifted himself by Deputy Doug, who gives him a break. When Eve shows up at Dawson's house later, she finally starts truth-talking, relating how the picture is her only link to her birth mother, who she is searching for. She confesses the caustic sex role she adopts means no-one can get close to her. Dawson says: "Well, once you get past the lying and the stealing and the using sex as a weapon, there's a lot of good stuff there." He confesses that he will miss her and she heads out.

Jack and Jen are stargazing when she admits to not being enamored with Henry. She treasures her friendship with Jack. "That's what's so great about you and me. Sex will never come between us." Henry's incapable of conversing with Jen and says to Jack: "If I opened my mouth, I'd hurl on her like that little kid on *South Park*." Jack contrives an "accidental" meeting which is a flop due to Henry's nerves and Jen's reminder that he's too young for her. To Jack she insists she is "... taking a break from deflowering the virgins of Capeside."

At Logan's Marina Joey's not impressed with Rob asking her out, and declines. He returns spruced for a date with ... Andie. When Rob tips Joey for filling up the boat, she returns the money telling him to keep it for "bail money". At the theatre later that evening, Andie expresses her joy to Joey about being on a date with Rob. Joey warns her about Rob but Andie dismisses her, saying: "Guys are hardly your area of expertise, is it Joey? I mean between Dawson and my gay brother..." Rather than desert Andie, Joey joins them, completely ruining their date. Next day, Rob callously fires Joey for closing early. Bessie's not pleased with the news.

At Grams' house, Dawson notices she has a picture of ... Eve's mother!

Episode Music

Chantal Kreviazuk – 'Before You'
Madonna – 'Swim'

Secrets and Lies · Episode #306
Written by Greg Berlanti & Alex Gansa
Directed by Greg Prange

Rob Logan would never have considered himself a pawn in someone else's chess game.

Dawson's history with secrets is none too good so he's surprised when a relaxed Jen says a secret will reveal itself when it is ready. At school, Jen's not so cool realising: "I'm turning into my mother." She feels the only reason she was elected Homecoming Queen is because "...I'm blonde and because I fill out my sweater." To top it off, Principal Green introduces Capeside High's previous 50 Homecoming Queens. Constance Freckling is 80 and old school in all senses of the term.

Dawson's pleasantly surprised his mom is in town for the homecoming celebrations, though tension still resides between Mitch and Gale. Dawson confides in his mom about Eve and the photo. He's obviously worried as the last time he possessed a secret like this, his soulmate dumped him. It turns out Gale's dream in Philadelphia turned sour when executives thought she was too old for the anchor position. Dawson reassures her and reckons she needs a friend – someone like Mitch, perhaps.

During the Homecoming Queen Garden Party, Jen's entrance in Goth gear nearly gives Constance Freckling a stroke. On top of that, Jen's entertainment is three drag queens, her point being: "Drag Queens, Homecoming Queens, what's the difference? It's just people dressing up, pretending they're something they're not." Henry confesses his love to Jen – but she gently rebuffs him, advising he find someone to reciprocate.

The Potter property is being converted into a bed-and-breakfast. Joey's worried but Pacey's reassurances quieten her nerves. It's funny, but didn't Dawson used to have this role? At school, Andie reveals to Joey that she's still seeing Rob, a contemptible character in Joey's eyes. When Joey later receives a distress call from Andie at Logan's household, she and Pacey collect the distraught girl. Transpires Rob was indecently forceful, leading Pacey to sock arrogant Rob. Andie's adamant about not filing a report; she simply needs to be alone – with Pacey. He shows her *True Love* which may not be Rob Logan's

Miss Freckling to Jen

(on setting an example as Homecoming Queen): "They're sweet, upstanding girls, who relish the chance to be role models. They tend to stand up straight, comb their hair, and wear brassieres!"

massive vessel, but it's perfectly formed. Andie takes the chance to make a move on Pacey who can't help but fold. The next morning he's full of regret, though Andie remains on cloud nine.

Rob is insistent he did nothing wrong – but Joey's not having it. When Joey discovers a bubbling Andie proclaiming her relationship with Pacey is back on, Joey's suspicious. When Andie finds Pacey ruminating last night's "mistake", she is devastated as only now had she glimpsed happiness since her hospital release. Andie is furious at Joey thinking she told Pacey about her Rob Logan suspicions. From Andie's look, it is obvious the tale was mostly fiction.

Episode Music

Meredith Brooks – 'Shout'

Natalie MacMaster – 'Get Me Through December'

The Weather Girls – 'It's Raining Men'

Bleach – 'Super Good Feeling'

Chantal Kreviazuk – 'Eve'

Escape from Witch Island .... Episode #307
Written by Tom Kapinos
Directed by James Whitmore, Jr.

Dawson and Joey play Mulder and Scully interpreting an old Capeside horror tale.

Dawson and Joey realize they've lost touch on the minutiae of their lives, so he invites her to help on a documentary he is making about the supposedly haunted Witch Island. Joey, as ever intuitive, says: "So basically you're ripping off *The Blair Witch Project*."

Dawson's footage features various Capeside residents recalling the Witch Island story. Jen's not buying it, insisting witch stories were all just a ruse to get rid of girls with a healthy sexual appetite. Watching Joey and Dawson walk off

together, Jen and Pacey wonder how it is that they never hooked up, "you'll find that the smartass sidekick never gets the girl," Pacey reckons.

Principal Green elucidates the tale from 1692 when 13 girls were banished to an island being suspected of witchcraft. They all died in a fire. The boatman on the way to the isle warns them not to get stranded there after dark. Wendy Dalrymple is their terminally chirpy guide. Jen tries out a spell on Pacey to make him love her – but Wendy catches them and is not amused.

Dawson:
"Joey, we're finally friends again. Why can't you just leave it alone?"

Wendy fills them in on Mary, the girl who was never found, banished to the island because of forbidden love. Joey says to Dawson the real movie should be about "soulmates torn apart by circumstances beyond their control." Dawson disagrees and they have a heartfelt conversation where they comment again on the lack of warmth in their relationship. The ferryman, nervous as a kitten at the approaching night, leaves the gang on the island.

The spell having been interrupted, Jen and Pacey enter into a mature contract to have sex – without any emotional nonsense. At the church where they're forced to spend the night, Jen and Pacey sneak off to try making out – but horrific sounds awaken all. Smoke billows, flames flicker, the teens stand wide-eyed, then flee with Dawson filming "Blair Witch" style. They use the ferryman's boat – which appears to be mysteriously awaiting them – to make their escape. The next day in class, the presentation goes well. Until that is, someone notices the eerie image on the screen!

Andie is filling her Pacey void with her role on the disciplinary committee. She follows rules to the letter, impressing Green with her verve, but he has to remind her that the since the Rules of Conduct were written in 1957, they're bound to be out of date.

Episode Music
Kim Stockwood – 'Puzzle Girl'
Tea Party – 'Gone'
Big Candy – 'If'

Reviewing his tape, Dawson and Joey play Mulder and Scully for us, Joey interpreting the flickering image logically as the antics of Wendy and the Boat Guy. Dawson apologizes to Joey for "taking our friendship for granted", and they have grown up just that little more.

Guess Who's Coming to Dinner? .... Episode #308
Written by Heidi Ferrer
Directed by Jim Charleston

Turkey, potatoes, pecan pie, and self-actualization are on the menu.

Pacey and Jen lament the failure of their Sex-No-Emotions deal while shopping for Thanksgiving. Everyone is heading over to Grams for dinner. On the surface, things are cosy in the Leery house, but Gale's looking for an apartment. Dawson confronts his parents about their false cheer. Holidays should also be about "honesty". They honestly tell him that their divorce has been finalized. At the Potter household, Bessie forgot to take the gizzards from the inside of the now roasting turkey, leaving Joey to wonder: "How could Mom be such a great cook, while we're so lame?" They reminisce about mom and Bessie regrets that her baby son Alexander never got to meet her.

Jen's ambivalent about her mother Helen's arrival in Capeside. She reveals to Grams that she's less than overjoyed: "Since she kicked me out of the house, we've had exactly one phone conversation." Helen tries to give Jen a pearl necklace but Jen feels Capeside's a little inappropriate for it. Jen confides her problems with her mom to Dawson who says: "She may have something to tell you." Joey reminds Jen how she still misses her deceased mom and gives the sullen teen reason to pause.

Dawson introduces himself to Helen and lets her know he's aware of Eve, her adopted daughter. Shocked, Mrs Lindley insists there's no need for Jen to know, now that Eve's left town. But Dawson warns Eve could turn up at any time and keeping family secrets like this has consequences.

Pacey did not expect Andie at the house and when he enquires how she is, out comes the heat, until Jack cools them down and reminds them of the occasion. Joey and Jack counsel Andie and Pacey respectively on their foundered relationship. They are assured that they think about and miss each other.

At mealtime, everyone gives thanks, with Jen's being particularly poignant: "I'd like to give thanks for second chances...

Joey to Jen: "We're all strangers to our parents, Jen. They love us, but they don't really know us. And sometimes before we get a chance to know them, they're gone."

For the opportunity to try and rebuild bridges that were once thought beyond repair." An overcome Helen has to excuse herself. She explains that the friendships Jen has made are the kind she has searched for in vain since leaving town. She confesses her tale and it transpires that Jen's "puritanical" dad still does not know about his own wife's teenage "indiscretion". Jen's horrified by the hypocrisy and says, "You are the most intensely selfish person I have ever known." She asks why her mother never phoned or visited – but Helen's answers show there 's no difference between an excuse and a reason. Jen tries it on with Pacey but the old pro recognizes "angry sex" when he sees it. He warns her not to despise her parents because they too have problems. Jen moves on to find her mother leaving and recognizes a troubled woman, who, at the age of 40 is frightened of being alone.

Episode Music

Ariel's Worm – 'Beginner's Luck'
Bree Sharp – 'America'
Mary Beth – 'Better Than Anyone'
Eurythmics – '17 Again'
Janis Ian – 'Getting Over You'
Alanis Morrisette – 'That I Would Be Good'

The episode ends with our gang of six recognizing they have not sat together as they are doing in a long while. "The group hug may be a little premature guys," warns Joey. "I'm sure we'll find a way to be estranged again in no time." Even Joey's comment cannot burst the bubble.

Four to Tango .... Episode #309
Written by Gina Fattore
Directed by James Whitmore, Jr

Two steps back, three steps forward. Keep that ass in and that chin up, people.

Jen and Pacey's Sex-No-Emotions agreement is fine, except there's no heat between them. While they are using Dawson's bedroom, Pacey's caught by Dawson though Jen escapes.

Mr Kapino, the new guidance counselor, warns Pacey about his failing grades, which are down to his loss of girlfriend/study pal Andie. Worried Pacey begs Joey's help with maths with the promise of "I'll do anything." Joey, who has been researching ways to win scholarship money, agrees. With her eyes on a ballroom dancing prize, she trades maths tips with Pacey for dancing class with dance teacher Penny.

At lunch, Andie is impressed by the pile of emails Jack got in response to the football story Dawson put on the web. While some are homophobic, one, from Ben Street, a gay guy who's also been through the wringer, offers support and they set up a date. But on return from his date, Jack reveals he was too scared to go in.

Searching his room, confused virgin Dawson finds a wrapped condom. When he mishears Pacey warning Joey no-one is to hear about the ballroom dancing, Dawson immediately jumps to sexy conclusions. When Jen walks into the video store seeking Pacey, Dawson talks about the condom and Jen pretends to know nothing. But when Dawson mentions

Jen to Pacey:
"And let's not forget we live in a society that thinks violence is cool but gets squeamish whenever two people who aren't of legal voting age start using correct names for their body parts."

the furtive chat with Joey, even she gets a little suspicious. Meanwhile Pacey has revealed to Joey that relationships with teacher Tamara and Andie have inadvertently taught him to expect sex as a study aid. Joey is uninterested and they head out to their dance club.

Jen and Dawson catch Joey and Pacey at dance class and realize Pacey IS regularly clutching Joey – but in a harmless way. Before they can escape they're corralled inside by teacher Penny. She reckons Dawson and Jen have much better form than the stiff Pacey and Joey who have "enough sexual tension to power a KISS reunion tour." They're all shocked. Musical partners means everyone gets a chance to talk – Dawson uses the chance to quiz Pacey about the condom. Even when Dawson gets the scholarship truth from Joey he still asks: "And that's all you and Pacey are to each other? Just friends?" Pacey and Dawson argue mid cha-cha-cha, with Pacey challenging his best friend's jealousy. (Pacey's done this before in the first season, Episode #110, *Double Date*.) Pacey warns Dawson that one day some guy will notice Joey and not ask Dawson's "permission". Pacey storms off closely followed by Jen. In the ballroom closet, they get a little frisky – only to get caught red-handed by Dawson and Joey. Disgusted Joey storms off, as does Dawson.

Jen shares an epiphany with Pacey. "Joey's definitely got something that attracts boys in emotional turmoil." Pacey is not having it until Jen spells out the attraction exists not between Jen and Pacey but Pacey and Joey.

Dawson reveals that even though he's the "ultimate romantic", as Joey puts it, he's not upset at Jen and Pacey's experiment, as it was not Joey in there. "Give 'em a break, Joey. They're just lonely." Joey's not having it as: "if a kiss is purely physical, if there's nothing else behind it, what's the point?" Wise Dawson tells her that those physical urges may be wrong without love to back them up, but they exist nonetheless. When Joey links up with Pacey again, forgiveness is in her eyes and their friendship has moved a step closer to... something more.

Episode Music
Violin Road – 'World You Want'
Peter Searcy – 'Hateful'
Vitamin C – 'Me, Myself & I'
Wood – 'Knock It On The Head'
Wood – 'Stay You'

First Encounters of the Close Kind ..... Episode #310
Written by Leslie Ray
Directed by Greg Prange

Anyone in art knows you need a tough skin to suffer the criticisms thrown your way.

With Dawson heading out to a film festival to show his movie *Escape From Witch Island*, and Joey heading out to a college, the air is scented with nerves. It could be an "amazing weekend" says Dawson. Trust Joey to add: "It could be the weekend all of our hopes and dreams came crashing down".

The university campus is bustling and Jack, Joey, and Dawson are overwhelmed. Andie has always wanted to go to this college and her perkiness knows no bounds. The group head off in different directions, with Jack off to do the tourist thing. At the Admissions office, Andie is efficient as ever and it turns out that her appointment isn't until MARCH! She pleads fruitlessly with

Fran the receptionist for an appointment to see the Dean. Fran's sympathetic advice is that the school will have little or no effect on Andie's life course.

Dawson's a little overwhelmed by the login process at the film festival and the brusque female, Nikki Green, entering his data does not help. They enter into a debate on the appeal of Spielberg and Dawson's in his element. During the screening of his movie, Dawson's practically nauseous and the mass exodus on the film's cessation doesn't help. Nikki later offers: "Your movie was way too derivative." Dawson, as we know, takes criticism like bitter medicine. Later, at another film screening, Dawson is impressed but much piqued that the movie turns out to be Nikki's. When Nikki does not win, it's up to Dawson to console her. "It was inspired Nikki. And it inspired me."

Joey discovers the student she has been paired up with is a guy – and a rude one at that (what is it with Boston?) A.J. Moller mocks Joey's distress to the point where she insists she can deal with the co-ed situation if he can. When Joey spots Dawson, she offers the consolation: "What do these hipper-than-thou film brats know anyway?" But Dawson's seriously dejected, doubting his big dream to be a movie director. At an English lecture later on, A.J. turns out to be the teaching assistant and royally humiliates Joey by trashing her favourite book, *Little Women*. He later apologizes and wins Joey over by taking her to the rare book room in the library and showing her a copy of *Little Women* once owned by its author Louisa May Alcott. The next day they part as friends, exchanging numbers.

On the train, Dawson meets Nikki, who turns out to be Principal Green's daughter. She's already in Mr Jordan's film class and is now looking forward to a little friendly competition. Dawson's face reveals he is a little less eager.

Jack, meanwhile, has been doing the Gay Tourist Thing and has wound up in a bar – for all of ten seconds. A predatory creep makes a move on him and he leaves with the speed we've seen on the football pitch. His baby steps towards his "gay" life move forward though, with a chance meeting with Ethan on the train home. Jack's surprised that this thing called Gaydar exists and older Ethan gives advice: "Treasure your innocence. Cherish it. Because once you lose it, it's gone forever."

Discussing the weekend, Joey's cynicism seems to have – temporarily, at least – been forgotten in Boston.

Joey:

"Everything in life is not about winning. You have to find joy in the process. You have to love what you do."

Episode Music

Ben Folds Five – 'Kate'
Counting Crows – 'Mrs Potter's Lullaby'
Last December – 'Run Into You'
Wood – 'Never Ending'

Barefoot at Capefest .... Episode #311
Written by Bonnie Schneider & Hadley Davis
Directed by Jan Eliasberg

How do you recover from the "let's just be friends" saying? Take the creek's advice and keep on flowing.

Jack and Jen are practically a married couple in their shopping habits. But Jack has his eye on Ethan who invites him to share a spot of grass (the sitting type) at Capefest, the alternative music er... fest. Next day, Jack turns up with

a reluctant Jen. When she finds Henry Parker, it's obvious he's still hurt from their last encounter. "For the past four weeks I've been giving you the silent treatment. And it didn't even register on your radar screen," he whines.

Ethan bolsters Jack's confidence. He's surprised their train chat was the first time Jack had even spoken to a gay kid – not including the Net. Ethan's smart: "Everyone always wants to define gay and straight by who you sleep with. It's not about that. It's about who and what you love." But Ethan's not smart enough to have kept an eye on his camping gear, which gets pilfered. Jen decides to return to her comfortable bed and leave Jack and Ethan to get acquainted, which scares Jack witless. Jack's attempt at a relationship with Ethan proves fruitless. He's a good guy though, and knowing Jack's not ready, he would not take it any further. They exchange numbers and leave it at that.

Mr Broderick to Andie
(about Pacey): "... the boy I know is an absolutely deplorable student. Has the ethics of a billy goat..."

As Jen is making her way through the crowd, who could that be singing so sweetly? None other than Henry. But he refuses to hear her compliments, especially as she never gave him a reason why she spurned his wooing. Jen reckons it was the age difference but Henry remains unhappy until she finally apologizes for "being careless with his heart."

Andie's super-efficiency wins her Assistant Director on the school play, under Mr Broderick. The auditions are a chance for her to shine – except Broderick wants Pacey to read for a part. Andie's face equals incredulity. She later tells him, "I want you to quit" but Pacey reveals Broderick will give him a C in English if he takes part in the play. During rehearsals, Pacey and Andie are tossed and turned through backflips of Broderick's direction. Next rehearsal, Broderick's absence leads to a crisp practice with great performances. Broderick tries to take credit, leaving Andie to storm out in disgust. Pacey encourages her to continue as he needs her, all she has to do is work around the anal Broderick.

Dawson continues to be foiled by Nikki in his film-making efforts and he's not happy. When he turns up at her door to complain about her nabbing the only good school camera, Principal Green invites him in for lunch. Eventually, Dawson and Nikki decide they could work together on her next project, a film about divorce and dysfunctional American families. Dawson offers this nugget: "our parents are... our primary example of love. And my primary example wasn't strong enough." Back home, Dawson starts removing his Spielberg posters – "The kid that hung these posters, I'm not him anymore." Dawson and Joey argue over their burgeoning friendships with others. Where once they would turn to each other for counsel, they seem to be confiding in others. Finally, they manage to repair hurt feelings with reminiscences about summers past.

Episode Music

Little Jinn – 'No Chance'
Rilo Kiley – 'The Frug'
Weekend Excursion – 'Finally Found You'
Rilo Kiley – '85'
Pete Stewart – 'Better Off'
Channeling Owen – 'Scared of Me'
Declan Nine – 'Dawson Capo'
Debra Davis – 'Angel In The Attic'
John Lennon – 'Imagine'

A Weekend in the Country .... Episode #312
Written by Jeffrey Stepakoff
Directed by Michael Katleman

Past memories give cause for concern.

Dawson, Pacey and Joey are watching *The Big Chill* at Joey's new bed-and-breakfast, which is worryingly empty. Joey blames Witter for inspiring this economic nightmare. At the bank, Bessie's so broke she considers mortgaging the house. Joey is not happy. Dawson aims to film the bed-and-breakfast and post it on the web. Pacey invites *Bed & Breakfast Quarterly*'s snobbish reviewer, Fred Fricke, and then invites a few neighbours to pretend that the house is filled to capacity. Dawson's thrown by the fact that Mitch and Gale are playing the part of a married couple. "Couldn't you've left my parents out of it?" he exclaims to Pacey.

Dawson confesses his confusion to Mitch and Gale. Mitch later confides to Dawson how difficult Gale is finding it, not being in work. He also explains that, though they're divorced, there's no time constraint on a couple caring about each other. Dawson apologizes to his mother for his self-obsession.

At school Henry invites Jen out in his own quirky way and she can't help but say yes. Jen describes him as a "child" to Grams though and she reckons that Henry would never be able to look at her the same were he to know her history – after all, Dawson didn't (Episode #103, *Discovery*).

A heart-to-heart enables Jen to ask Dawson why he was so scared of her past. He answers: "... anything that we don't know or understand can scare us." He knows now he was wrong. Jen confesses her "... laundry list of sexual crimes" to Henry and is surprised by his mature attitude.

Dawson to Joey and Pacey:
"I've taken down the Spielberg posters in my room. Everything's in question lately."

Pressured though Andie is with schoolwork and her Assistant Director role on the play, we know she loves it. Jack refuses Andie's persistent attempts to make him move home – it's his dad he is trying to avoid, not his sister. While helping Joey and Bessie with their bed-and-breakfast launch, Andie raises the subject again – much to Jack's chagrin. It's only when she's over at Jen's house that Andie realizes how at home Jack is there. She finally divulges how much she has missed him.

Bessie and Joey are bending over backwards attempting to accommodate the burdensome Fred Fricke. The furnace is cold while Joey and Bessie's debate is red hot. Joey is angry at having no say in familial proceedings while Bessie's angry over trying to raise two kids on her own while Alexander's dad, Bodie, works out of town.

Grams impresses the bed-and-breakfast crowd by lighting a fire which then has everyone reminiscing on their favourite smells. Joey's memories of her mother's hopes of opening a bed-and-breakfast bring her to tears – and to admit to Mr Fricke that the guests are fakes.

Episode Music

Julie Plug – 'Starmaker'
Bryan Kelley – 'Fear'
Weekend Excursion – 'Getting By'
Kind of Blue – 'Will You Ever Know'
Pancho's Lament – 'Absence Of An Angel'
Pancho's Lament – 'Promise Me This'
Joni Mitchell – 'Both Sides Now'

When Joey wakes up the next morning, Dawson, Pacey, Jen, Andie and Jack are all cooking breakfast. At table, Joey's surprised to find Mr Fricke – who's impressed by the warmth of the house. But not as impressed as Joey when Bodie surprises her. The brother-in-law can throw down in the kitchen!

The reminiscences have worked on the not-so-estranged Leerys as well. Mitch reminds Gale of the dream they once had of opening a restaurant. Gale is hesitant... but her interest is piqued. Dawson, meanwhile, tells Pacey he's changed from being "glib, lazy, predictable" to something else. He thanks Pacey for taking care of Joey as well as he has. "I'm happy she has you."

Northern Lights .... Episode #313
Written by Gina Fattore
Directed by Jay Tobias

The Northern Lights in Capeside? There's stranger to come.

Pacey persuades a reluctant Joey to help him rehearse his lines from *Barefoot in the Park*. But on opening night, she won't be there as she has a date with A.J. for a rare chance to see the Northern Lights. Pacey reckons A.J.'s after a look at Joey's lights. In rehearsal at school, Pacey's forgetfulness has Andie twitching with nerves – which get worse when it turns out Mr Broderick's hypochondria is working overtime, and he's leaving her in charge.

The big night finds Pacey panicking about forgotten lines (but still noticing how fine Joey looks for her date). He tries to persuade Joey to stand the guy up – but she's having none of it. Back at school, it's up to Dawson to find the missing lead and pep talk him into following what he enjoys – acting. After all, Dawson has given up film class – much to Nikki's chagrin – but he is happy to widen his dreams a little. Pacey's surprised Dawson's so cool – considering Joey's date. Oops.

Henry's been avoiding Jen, thinking she's cancelling his hard-worked-for-date. Jen is actually postponing because it's Pacey's opening night. Henry invites himself along despite Jen's concealed misgivings. No smile on Henry's face

Dawson:
"Joey can take care of herself."
Pacey:
"This is Joey we're talking about. You remember her? The girl who's destiny is intrinsically linked with yours?"

when, at the play, he discovers Grams. Pleasant lady, but not whom he wanted to put his arm across. Pacey is great on stage, wowing the crowd – especially Henry – with his comedic timing.

At the Northern Lights "party" a lot of mathematical nerds are milling around. As A.J. snatches the alcoholic beverage away from Joey she quips, "I thought that's what college guys lived for, opportunities to get high-school girls all liquored up." A.J. takes Joey aside and confesses to loving the magical Capeside – though Joey cannot agree. Their discussion on teenage ambition lightens Joey's concerns about her future. She's acutely afraid of failure. When A.J. makes a move, Joey gets uncomfortable and says: "I kinda promised someone I'd be somewhere."

At the after-play party, Andie and actors are hailed as successes. Jen approaches a lonesome looking Pacey to congratulate him and commiserate that Joey wasn't there to see his success. But she turns up, and Pacey is more than a little relieved. Nikki finds Dawson to tell him that he is "taking this whole precocious teenager thing a bit too far." Dawson relates his first viewing of *Jurassic Park*, when a couple made out throughout the movie. He is older now but not the making-out type of guy, not the wide-eyed kid but a third type who deconstructs rather than enjoys a film.

Joey explains to Pacey why she is no longer on the date – he has guessed A.J. kissed her (smudged lipstick is a big clue to a guy with two cops in the family). Joey is not likely to pursue the relationship for a number of reasons. Pacey's wisdom impresses her: "You know, life may surprise you yet, Joey Potter. You love someone, it doesn't work out, you think it'll never happen again, but it does. I guarantee you it does." Henry confronts Jen about their "date". "You're embarrassed to be here with me." He later clambers to a height to make Jen say something worthwhile to him – mirroring Pacey's character in the play. It does not end the same though – as Jen makes him realize this is real life and refuses to say the words he desires to hear from her. Back on terra firma, Jen realizes Henry has this wonderfully naïve attitude that everything will be all right. She, on the other hand, is "fond of my old pals disappointment and deceit. They're so reliable." But she kisses him – 100% truthfully.

When the Northern Lights finally reveal themselves – Joey sees them with Dawson. In her delightful way, she thinks the timing "typical".

Episode Music
Savage Garden – 'Affirmation'
Sue Medley – 'No Regrets'
Pancho's Lament – 'Get On The Bus'
Trina Hamlin – 'Even Now'
Sinead Lohan – 'What Can Never Be'

The Valentine's Day Massacre .... Episode #314
Written by Tom Kapinos
Directed by Sandy Smolan

Valentine's is often a lot more hellish than the angelic card and flower sellers could ever imagine.

Dawson's "condescending" driving lessons have Joey on edge. Peacemaker Pacey invites Joey out with him and Dawson for a Valentine's evening, namely Matt Caufield's party. Matt's apparently a jerk of another tribe and Joey will have none of it.

Love-struck Henry donates too much blood to raise money for his date with Jen. The lady pretends to be jaded but really, she's anxious. Wobbly Henry keels over during the meal yet, en route to hospital, confesses his plasma donation and gives Jen the gift, a ring, which is much too small for her finger. Grams' pearl of wisdom to Jen stresses Henry's struggling to be something he isn't. Jen and Henry agree to be themselves in future.

Jack's not buoyant that Andie has invited his ex-girlfriend Kate to spend time with them. She does not know he is gay, but Andie reckons Kate will understand. Jack on the other hand likens her to "Ally McBeal on angel dust." On her arrival, everyone sees what he means when she reveals her last boyfriend broke up with her because he was gay! Jack has not even had time to reveal his sexuality to her. Pacey decides troubled Kate and Dawson would make a great couple – even though Joey changes her mind and decides to come to the party. Privately, she confesses to Pacey that Dawson is "aimless and adrift".

Bacchanalian Matt menaces the likes of our gang by reputation alone. His party is on a golf course and swinging fully when the crew arrives. Matt eyes up an unimpressed Joey. As Ms Potter privately moans about Pacey to Andie, the observant ex-girlfriend says that Joey sounds like she did "before I started dating him." Even though Joey's driving a golf cart, they get pulled over by Doug.

During a private walk, Kate believes she's seen through the charade and identified Dawson as the gang's good guy. He's annoyed: "Maybe, just maybe,

Pacey to Joey (about Dawson – who's right there!): "It's a party! Is our boy not entitled to a moment or two in which he transcends his miserable, angst-ridden existence and actually enjoys himself?"

I'm here to take advantage of your situation." Kate's mirth-filled. "If you don't wanna be a nice guy, Dawson, when you take a girl into the woods, don't talk to her about kissing her. Kiss her." He does. She stops him, then vomits.

In a holding cell, Jack confesses to Kate. While everyone braces themselves for the emotional onslaught, she merely laughs before checking Dawson's leanings. "Because apparently only gay guys will kiss me." Joey is not amused and neither is Dawson at her response, "... you have got to start letting me make some mistakes."

When a still-drunk Pacey adds a few mean comments of his own, Joey accuses him of being hurtful to her all night. He reveals annoyance at their weekly dance of being soulmates and then seeming enemies. Everyone else is released, Pacey is left inside. Of all people, Pacey reveals his feelings for Joey to Doug – who actually gives good counsel "... you don't come across that many people who have the ability to give you butterflies."

Episode Music

Patria – 'Passion'
Universal Honey – 'Real World'
Bryan Kelley – 'Charming The Gods'
DJ Rap – 'Bad Girl'
Beanbag – 'Taste Test'
Julie Plug – 'What Can I Say'
Chevelle – 'Point #1'
Debra Davis – 'The Way Things Used To Be'
Susan Agluklark – 'Never Be The Same'

Mitch had let Dawson off the smashed boat incident lightly – but not this time. Dawson's informed that he will be working at the restaurant Gale is planning to buy.

Pacey takes up the gauntlet and starts teaching Joey to drive. From her laughter, it's clearly going better than it did with condescending Dawson.

Crime and Punishment .... Episode # 315
Written by Gina Fattore & Alex Gansa
Directed by Joe Napolitano

Pacey's habit of appearing before the disciplinary committee is getting dangerous.

Joey's Capeside High mural of a Chinese figure does not, in Pacey's eyes, capture Principal Green's request for school spirit. Her explanation, "art has power" is apparently lost on Pacey. Next morning, Dawson attempts to ease Joey's mural unveiling nerves. She will be baring her soul and wonders how the school will react.

Andie treats her position on the Capeside High Disciplinary Committee earnestly. Matt Caufield is "on trial" for cheating charges and while Andie favors hours of detention, Green's happy with a warning. Green later reveals Andie's phenomenal practice SAT scores and she's all smiles till he tells her she has to do it again. This will be a tough one, Andie thinks, without an answer sheet. Next day, she tenders her Disciplinary Committee resignation, claiming she is not the person Green thinks she is. Andie later confesses to her brother that she was the practice SAT culprit and how she aims to tell the Principal to ease her conscience.

Matt Caufield to Principal Green:

"I'm rich. I'm smart. That's all the possibility I need."

Looking for a place to stay, Pacey tries Doug. "This is not *Party of Five*," the neat freak wails. Pacey informs him their sister Kerry and her kids are in town so he has no room at the Witter Inn.

The other artists' mural speeches are toe-curling but receive polite applause. Joey's is as smart as ever, but when her mural is uncovered we see it has been defaced. Outside, Pacey's convinced it was a personal attack while Dawson thinks it was merely vandalism. Later, Dawson suggests repainting but Joey's scornful, prompting him to call her "... defeated, demoralised, dejected ..." but alliteration does not impress her. Dawson adds she's probably relieved at not having her work judged and walks out.

Pacey impresses as an undercover agent, finding out that Matt's most likely to have done it. Pacey and Matt get into a vicious fight. As soon as Pacey has the upper hand, Principal Green shows up, furious. It is Dawson who defies Pacey to reveal the whole sordid incident, though Matt still proclaims his innocence. But Dawson stylishly grills Matt until he trips himself up. He then admits it. "It was ugly, for one thing. An eyesore."

Later, Joey arrives at Doug's to berate Pacey: "If you're gonna throw away your future, do it on your own account." Pacey's anger at this leads him to reveal he was only looking out for Joey since Dawson asked him a while back. Joey's face – read devastated.

Next day, Matt's expulsion stuns him. Dawson's also stunned at Joey's anger at what she calls his "... little wife-swapping arrangement". It's Dawson's turn to tell some home truths, though, when he asks how Joey cannot see that Pacey obviously cares for her. She pauses thoughtfully. When Pacey exits the "trial" his demeanour suggest he's been saved from the chopping block. Instead of

Episode Music

suspension, Principal Green has put him in the Capeside Mentoring program.

Andie follows through, and unburdens her heart to Green. He's disappointed but stresses how different she is from the likes of Matt Caufield. Joey cannot help but be pleased at Pacey's help with the mural. They are back to their banter and bickering, but that's them at their best.

To Green With Love .... Episode #316
Written by Gina Fattore & Greg Berlanti
Directed by Ken Fink

The radioactive fallout from Caufield's expulsion continues to fall acidically.

Robert Caufield – Matt's father – makes waves, coercing Superintendent Fielding to make Principal Green change his mind about Matt's expulsion. It works – Green has the week to reconsider or resign.

Dawson, Pacey, Joey, and Green's daughter Nikki cannot fathom the town's thinking. Joey feels muted by the adult's attitude to students and though Pacey recommends she rallies the students, it's mellifluous A.J. she listens to.

Gale greets Sherry, her young, pretty but somewhat naïve TV station successor. Sherry's report stuns all as it's blatantly biased against Green. Joey holds a meeting and Pacey – a veteran at school politics – offers to help, but A.J.'s already on the scene.

Jen to Pacey:
"... are you gonna let hurt feelings and pride prevent you from actually being the friend you so innocently purport yourself to be?"

Gale's restaurant is soon to open. She and Dawson discuss Joey's fighting plans and Gale can foresee difficulties with partisan Sherry providing television coverage. Dawson persuades his mother to cover the story herself. Once Gale's started though, a threatened Sherry turns up and almost goes brunette with shock when Joey frostily dismisses her.

Superintendent Fielding summons Joey to inform her of his displeasure at her rabble picketing his office. Joey threatens him with a 300-strong petition and a student protest the following night – both of which are currently pure fiction. Back at the Potter Bed-and-Breakfast Pacey warns Joey against such bluffs. But with A.J.'s support, Joey's on cloud ten. Joey kissing A.J. equals heartache for Pacey. He confides in Jen: "I'm sorta falling ... for the worst person I could ever have fallen for."

Bessie receives a call warning her against letting campaigning students use the Potter Bed-and-Breakfast. "We can't afford to antagonize the people who hold the mortgage on this house," she warns. Joey insists they fight on as the town is actually up in arms because Principal Green is black.

The Leery reporting team's interview with Fielding is interesting as he purports that firing Green is "what's best for this community". Gale surprises him with his contract under which he's supposed to pursue student interests – and the students back Green!

Nikki heads out to the rally, let down by dad's reticence despite all the people who support him. Even Joey's surprised at how many supporters turn up and gets a little unnerved at having to address them. Instead of a tirade against the system, individuals simply step to the microphone to praise Green. Nikki's heartfelt speech is underlined by her father's surprise attendance. He informs all he will be leaving, but his last lesson is about individuals harnessing their individual powers.

The day of departure finds Joey in Principal Green's office, where he is packing up. "I can't help feeling like I failed you." He, though, has never felt more successful. The student body lines the hallways clapping and cheering.

Gale's story will be run on the local station. She's chuffed but gives due praise to her son. "No matter how much you think you've changed, you're still the quiet hero, Dawson."

Pacey, meanwhile is proving heroic himself. He has rented a wall for Joey to paint. She's stunned but highly appreciative.

Episode Music

Pete Stewart – 'Better Off'
Savage Garden – 'Two Beds and a Coffee Machine'
Mary Beth – 'Tracks of My Tears'
James Taylor – 'That Lonesome Road'

Cinderella Story .... Episode #317
Written by Jeff Stepakoff
Directed by Janice Cooke-Leonard

Those fellas with females as best friends are best handled carefully.

Joey's invitation to an awards ceremony where A.J. will be reading some of his work has her and Pacey excited – if for different reasons. He insists her long-distance relationship lacks reality. She does not concur. In Boston, Joey's greeted not by A.J. but by Morgan, A.J.'s best friend. A.J. and Morgan's

banter is bubbling, their friendship deep as tree roots. "Why didn't you tell me about her?" Joey later enquires. "You have nothing to worry about." Morgan's like A.J.'s secretary/wife in that she often knows better than he does what's good for him.

In a private conversation, Joey learns that Morgan and A.J. have indeed kissed: "...afterwards we both knew it was silly and weird." Joey invites Morgan along to the presentation and Morgan's appreciative: "...I was a little wary about meeting you. But I honestly could not have imagined a better woman to see him with. You're all right Joey Potter."

Pacey's weekend is community-service themed. His mentee is Buzz Thompson, nine years old and already a smartass. "I'm

Pacey to Joey!
"... all you have is an eyes-closed wish made by a girl who doesn't see the reality right in front of her."

not like you, Pussy," Buzz warns. Pacey sets Buzz to work on his boat. Conversation is prickly but Pacey learns that Buzz's dad died. Spying the boat's name, *True Love*, Buzz enquires about "the girl", disbelieving Pacey's claim that there isn't one. "... you can't tell a girl how you feel about her. You're pathetic." Time to go home kid, Pacey decides. He complains at the community centre but decides to stick at it. Witter is not a quitter. At Buzz's house, the kid is quietly appreciative of the attention – though reluctant to show it. They connect. Buzz admits his father is not deceased and Pacey is able to says the name "Joey" aloud.

At the ceremony, A.J.'s reading concerns friends falling in love. It's not at all lost on Joey. Privately, she tells A.J. that "Morgan is your muse," and encourages him to pursue something more. He's honestly heartbroken: "God, Joey! Give me a chance," but then he quietly acquiesces. In her time of need, Joey calls Pacey to pick her up.

Gale's restaurant would be ready to open if it had staff, menus, fixtures, fittings, or a name. Dawson ropes Jack and Andie into taste-testing for him while he hires Jen as a waitress. It's just a shame she can barely carry a tray. When Mitch arrives, Gale's none too pleased. He's worthy and wise but leaves little space for Gale to learn. Dawson receives her wrath and he, upset, reminds her how she taught him to ask for help when needed. Why is she finding it so difficult to follow her own advice? Dawson departs.

Jen's observation to him hits the mark: "You're trying to put your family back together, Dawson." Though he understands they're unlikely to be a family unit again, he finds it difficult to accept.

Next morning, Dawson's greeted by an apologetic but beaming Gale. Changes are afoot; she's hired Mitch as a manager, gone into partnership with chef Bodie, and decided Jen's a better hostess than waitress.

Joey's reticence lasts most of the drive home. It's the next morning when she explains to Pacey: "You were right. Right as always." Joey realizes only Dawson and Pacey have ever really known her. This floors Pacey who, unable to articulate his words, kisses her. Planets stop their revolutions round distant suns. (See Episode #201, *The Kiss*, for Dawson and Joey's first kiss.)

Episode Music

Sue Medley – 'Gone'

Dag Juhlin – 'I Can't Try Hard Enough'

Brooke Ramel – 'The Answer'

Tara MacLean – 'Dryland'

Kind of Blue – 'I Know'

Tara MacLean – 'Settling'

Neverland .... Episode #318
Written by Maggie Friedman
Directed by Patrick Norris

Even once lips part, kisses can linger forever and a day.

Joey participates in the kiss but does not actively reciprocate. When Pacey's finished she whacks him repeatedly then hisses: "How could you take a simple declaration of friendship as an invitation to maul me?" A distraught Pacey tries to play it off as an "impulse". She's bubbling with fury and reminds him that because of Dawson, it couldn't be just an impulse. They part infuriated.

Joey and Pacey relate the incident to their siblings with mixed reactions. Bessie's outraged. Doug's intrigued. Both, though, understand Joey and Pacey's fear about Dawson discovering.

Jack's pleased his pal Ethan is coming to stay until Andie informs him that their dad isn't going on his business trip after all. Jack takes a stance, bulldozing his dad's early attempt to send Ethan home. Their father plays pleasant host but Jack reckons all he's doing is spying. Ethan seems oblivious and even invites Mr McPhee out to dinner with him and Jack. Ethan wows McPhee senior with his personality but Jack's furious and upsets his dad who says mournfully: "I'm trying ... but I guess I'm just not the father you want. Or need." Jack never expected his father to be the first-move maker and they begin to release some of their anger, and relate to each other as father and son should.

Joey to Bessie:
"I'm sick of being defined by my relationships with boys in my life – I mean – when do I get to figure out who I am?"

At school, Dawson's concerned with the bulldozing of the woods he and Pacey used to play in. Seeing it as an opportunity to unburden his heart, Pacey invites him camping one last time. Reminiscing on childhood memories the boys are scared witless by Buzz and two of his pals. The little ones finally fall asleep, allowing Pacey a chance to talk. He opts not to confess but instead stresses how important his friendship with Dawson is. Leery feels the same way about Pacey and Joey: "...she's my conscience, my soulmate, my inspiration..." Trust him to unwittingly lay the guilt on thick and heavy.

Jen's taken aback by Henry doing the family thing for his birthday, then annoyed when she discovers only she is excluded. Andie senses stress clouds over Jen and Joey, and coaxes them into a girl's night out. A private moment and Jen confides to Joey that her counsel is there if needed: "You, me, Dawson, Pacey – it's a real incestuous group." Joey does not want to talk. At a roller rink the girls bond. Jen, though, notices a kid's party which transpires to be –

Henry's! Everyone is agape at sexily dressed Jen. Privately, Henry says his childish birthday parties merely humiliate him – he couldn't force that on Jen. She forgives. Back home, Joey confides to Jen about the oh-so-awful Pacey kiss but Jen says she doth protest too much, deepening the frown in Joey's brow. Next morning, Joey finds Pacey to say the kiss need not mean anything, if they make nothing of it. They both agree – but with reluctance.

Episode Music

Trina Hamlin – 'In My Life'
Mission Delores – 'Give Me A Reason'
Brooke Ramel – 'Anything'
Last December – 'If You Leave'
Eli – 'I'll Stay Right Here'
Leona Naess – 'Chosen Family'
Edwin McCain – 'Go Be Young'
Trina Hamlin – 'Even Now'

Stolen Kisses .... Episode #319

Written by Tom Kapinos
Directed Greg Prange

We build our own histories which are not always easy to look back upon.

Spring Break sees Joey, Andie, Pacey, and a friend of his called Will making a road trip to visit Dawson's Aunt Gwen. Joey has met her before and describes her as an incredibly talented painter/teacher who "lives life on her own terms." Gwen's indeed an earth child who welcomes all with open arms. Lack of space means Joey and Pacey have to bunk together – uneasily. (See Episode #112, *Decisions*, for the first time Joey and Dawson bunked together.)

At the town's pool hall, the supposedly rusty players Pacey and Will hustle some locals out of some green with their skills – much to Andie's surprise.

Jen to Shelly (who's pawing Henry): "Get your boobs away from him!"

That night, Andie and Will share a moment as he confides his home-life problems to her. A little later, Pacey gets Andie to admit that she may like Will. The feeling of 'moving on' is a mix of emotions for this pair.

Meanwhile, out shopping, Gwen's antennae senses the coolness between Joey and Dawson, and they're forced to relate their past history. Later, Joey assures Dawson that he has matured, but he surprises her with: "I'm starting to forget why... we're not together."

At Leery's Fresh Fish, Gale's inundated by bills but luckily, also guests. An old friend, Megan, turns up and relates how her husband Tom – Mitch's best man no less – died in a car accident. Gale doesn't tell Megan she and Mitch have divorced and Megan gives them the speech Tom had made at their wedding. Mitch resists reading it but eventually does, and even digs out their wedding video. It's painful but gives them a chance to remember the magic.

Henry is now working at the restaurant, and, to Jen's annoyance, a waitress called Shelly starts making a move on him. When Henry accuses Jen of being jealous, sarcasm rules: "Oh puhleaze. I am so not in touch with that emotion." But when Jen catches Shelly pawing Henry, she explodes: "I've looked all over the place for one like him, and I'm not giving him up without a fight." Such an eruption of emotion forces Jen to later admit tearfully to Henry that he has her heart.

During karaoke evening everyone pushes Dawson and Joey into performing their duet, the Monkees' "Daydream Believer". Their shared history is deep and affects Pacey to the point where he exits stage left. Joey follows and admits their agreement that the first kiss meant nothing is cheap baloney. "I'm gonna kiss you, Potter," Pacey warns before doing so. The kiss lasts forever, or at least until Gwen rounds the corner and catches them. Gwen tells Joey to follow her heart but, "don't be reckless with someone else's emotions." Joey leaves to try and tell Dawson, but it's impossible. Later, she and Pacey acknowledge how strong their feelings are by kissing again.

Episode Music

Better Days – 'Walking In My Sleep'
X – 'Wild Thing'
Better Days – 'One & Only'
Shivaree – 'Goodnight Moon'
Shivaree – 'Idiot Waltz'
Mary Beth – 'Daydream Believer'

The Longest Day .... Episode # 320
Written by Gina Fattore
Directed by Perry Lang

Of repetition and realization. Of repetition and realization. Of repetition and realization.

Act One: Pacey's *True Love* is ready to launch. Giggly, happy, wracked with guilt, Joey and Pacey ponder how to tell Dawson. Pacey searches all day for an elusive Dawson and back at Doug's he's surprised at his brother's insistence that he drop Joey. "... you're just going to trade a lifelong friend for some teen romance?" Later, Pacey bumps into Joey on the Leery property and is stunned that she reflects Doug's sentiment – wanting to wait to make sure their love is bona fide. Dawson interrupts the ensuing row and Pacey deep breathes then spills the beans!

Grams, away for a night, warns Jen against having Henry over at the house. Jen promises to obey, but with a glint in her eye. Will never went home after

Spring Break. Andie has him hooked. At the library, he asks her for a date and she accepts.

Act Two: The gang prepare to launch *True Love*. Says Joey to Jen: "... so many of my feelings have been clouded over by my fear of what Dawson will do..." but she's sticking with the plan for Pacey to confess later that day. Jen's got a night planned with Henry despite Grams' warning.

Andie tells Joey about her expectant date with Will: "... he has no idea how cute he is. Which is key. God save us from the ones who do..." Trouble is though, she's not completely over Pacey! Joey feels the guilt.

Joey opts to tell Dawson herself. But he's watching *The Last Picture Show* which they watched on their first date. Joey just can't do it and departs, distraught. She meets Pacey, they repeat their row, Dawson interrupts, and he is told the news. He calmly says: "I know."

Dawson to Joey:

"And if you choose him, I won't be there to pick up the pieces when it falls apart."

Act Three: Dawson brings the bottle of champagne for the launch of *True Love*, giving Pacey valuable words of praise. At the library Will explains to Dawson how cool it is that Pacey accepts the idea of he and Andie dating.

Henry's not in Grams' house but he is on the porch. Dawson pops over and Jen is suspiciously consoling, not realizing he knows nothing! His curiosity has been awakened now but though he's insistent, Jen's resilient. Dawson pauses, brow furrowed, as he skilfully deconstructs the recent events and Joey's bizarre behaviour. Things fall into place. Back home, Mitch holds him as he breaks down.

Later, Joey pops through the window and they chat again about the movie, but this time we see Dawson's barely keeping everything under control. The movie ends up, he says, with "Everybody hating each other. Everybody alone." It's no surprise Joey couldn't confess to him at that moment in time.

Once again, Dawson reveals to Pacey and Joey: "I know." But he adds: "Jen... thought I knew. But then, I'd have to be pretty stupid not ... to have realized that the two people I trusted most in the world were lying to me." Andie interrupts and Dawson doesn't hesitate in quickly bringing her up to speed.

Take four: Henry takes his comforting of Jen too far. She's upset at her mistake and he's clasping? She throws him out.

Andie's date goes swimmingly until she interrupts the gang mid-explosion. All she can say to Pacey is: "Joey's never gonna love you the way she loves Dawson."

Episode Music

Jennifer Parsignault – 'Matter of Time'
Dido – 'Thank You'
Eagle Eye Cherry – 'Miss Fortune'
Jann Arden – 'Mend'
Jann Arden – 'In Your Keeping'

Dawson and Joey have a private chat where Dawson's incredulity reaches new heights. It's ultimatum time: "You don't get to have us both... This ruins everything Joey." After Joey's departure, Jen enters and, exhausted, Dawson tells her ominously: "You can fight for what you want."

On the pier, Pacey and Joey realize it's over. "It has to be" Joey says mournfully.

Show Me Love . . . . Episode #321
Written by Liz Tigelaar & Holly Henderson
Directed by Morgan J. Freeman

The sailing terms "jibe" and "tack" take on a whole new meaning.

Two things have gripped Capeside, boat race fever and loneliness. Friendships are rent asunder, school is a nightmare. Dawson's the first-move maker but chooses to have Joey, not Pacey, in his life. She, though, is wracked by guilt.

At Leery's Fresh Fish, Gale enlightens Dawson on the restaurant's sponsorship of Pacey in the Capeside Regatta. Dawson finds Pacey to give him a banner but the exchange is terse. Pacey says to his racing partner Will afterwards: "I was his best friend – as long as I wasn't a threat to him."

Dawson is a late entry to the race (with Jack in the McPhee boat) sponsored by Potter Bed-and-Breakfast. The sponsor prize – front page of the Capeside Tourism Brochure – would be a great business boost but is that an ulterior motive Joey can smell? With Mitch helping his son, he at least has a chance.

Henry begs Jen to forgive his roaming hands but she relents only after much puppy dog eyes from him. The apology is underlined by a beautiful rooftop picnic and Henry's attempt

Pacey to Joey:
"Don't you get it? No matter what I do, Dawson wins. If I drop out, he wins. If I race, I'm forced into competing with him. If I win that race, I beat... you. And guess who wins?"

to be the most "original" guy in her life. Jen innocently spends the night looking at scenery but Grams is furious to see Jen "slip back" into her old ways. Jen exits in disbelief. Later, Grams acknowledges her maturity and offers to have the safe sex chat with her.

Will gives Andie some things to think about as he's leaving town to pursue his scholarship and reckons Pacey could do with a friend. Pacey's old friend, Joey, asks him to drop out of the race and when he declines, to try harder to repair things with Dawson. Leery isn't hearing it though: "Do you think you can compete with history?" he spits. And they get ready to rumble.

During Dawson and Pacey's sea battle, Joey reminds Andie what it's like to make a mistake and lose someone you love. The regatta peaks with stubborn Dawson failing to acknowledge Pacey's right of way and getting disqualified. Joey says to the furious pair: "... nothing is worth going through this." Dawson snatches a private moment to confess to Joey: "I want you more than I ever have," but all Joey needs is his friendship.

Episode Music

Nik Kershaw – 'Fiction'
Better Days – 'Sunday Morning'
Jill Sobule – 'Somewhere In New Mexico'
Megadeth – 'Crush Em'
Switchfoot – 'Let That Be Enough'
Troy Young Campbell – 'Hazel'
Jenny Bruce – 'Music To My Ears'

The public declarations of love have roused Mitch and Gale from their estranged stupor and they realize there's still passion between them. Joey brings a Spielberg movie for Dawson and it would appear that bruised hearts and egos are slowly healing all over Capeside.

The Anti-Prom . . . . Episode #322
Written by Maggie Friedman
Directed by Greg Prange

Those who don't remember the past are condemned to repeat it ...

It's finals and Junior Prom time. Dawson and Joey agreed long ago that if neither had a date they would go to the Prom together as friends. Mitch and Gale, however, are doing more than friends and Mitch confides in Dawson about his hope of reconciliation. Mitch confronts Gale to make a decision about their relationship.

Aiming to go to the Prom with Ethan, Jack has to deal with homophobic Barbara Johns who refuses him tickets asking if he intends to dance "... stubbled cheek to stubbled cheek?" Andie wants to fight, but Jack's ambivalent. Dawson muses and the idea of the Anti-Prom takes shape. Next day, Jack and Andie have their own table selling tickets next to Barbara. Their line is filled with kids out of the ordinary, whom Barbara endearingly refers to as the "dregs of society".

Pacey reckons the recent emotional tumult is most regretful because he hurt Andie, so asks her to the Anti-Prom. During their preparations, Jen has a prom-sex talk with Henry and advises they make the decision now – "Not to do it."

Departing for the prom, Joey's a lot more uncomfortable than Dawson, who relishes Bessie taking snaps – especially since he loaned Joey his mother's diamond earrings. Andie and Pacey's arrival heightens tension. When Jack first met Ethan, the older lad related how he went to his prom with a guy but he now admits the story is fiction, much to Jack's annoyance. Ethan admits his feelings for Jack but insists Jack is not ready – which indeed, Jack proves, as he cannot bring himself to kiss Ethan.

When Jen discovers – in the middle of the Prom – that Henry is going to football camp for two months, she stuns him with the admission that the no-sex talk was a ruse to take the pressure off him. They decide to call it quits and head their separate ways.

Dawson to Joey:
"Call me an eternal optimist but I have faith. If there's one thing that kiss last night showed me, it's this – you're the one for me, Joey."

Episode Music

Julie Plug – 'In Every Corner'

Wild Colonials – 'This Misery'

Heather Nova – 'London Rain'

Wild Colonials – 'It's Not Unusual'

Granian – 'Foresight'

Kind of Blue – 'I Believe'

Twila Paris – 'Once In A Life'

Sarah Siaan – 'My Invitation'

Chantal Kreviazuk – 'Little Things'

On the dancefloor, Joey's a little tired of the dagger eyes Pacey and Dawson are making at each other and departs. Jack counsels her to do whatever feels right. And dancing with Pacey makes Joey feel right (remember the lessons?) Spotting Dawson though, she can almost see his heart break and runs after him. He admits he wanted to win her heart not just her friendship.

Andie's is another heart which has been hurt. Walking her home, Pacey tells her he is sailing to Key West over the summer. Andie encourages him to really, truly tell Joey how he feels. As ever, the adults have also been struggling with their feelings but finally, finally, Gale asks Mitch to marry her!

True Love .... Episode #323

Teleplay by Tom Kapinos & Gina Fattore
Directed by James Whitmore, Jr.

Summer beckons enticingly, as does love.

Dawson and Joey – as best man and bride of honour – have responsibilities, least of all to get on. Dawson is managing but we sense a little uneasiness with Joey. Mitch and Gale are all loved up as they prepare to re-tie the knot. Jack's telephone impression – relaying messages between a truculent pair called Henry and Jen – solves little.

Doug's concerned about Pacey's sea quest, as he's not told Joey he's going nor how he truly feels about her. Doug takes it upon himself to enlighten her. Joey's confrontation leads to Pacey saying: "...our being or not being together is your choice." She responds that she may have asked for time, but he is the one giving up. Pacey makes an analogy that it is the same way she has given up on her wall.

Pacey to Doug:

"This is what happens when the male brain is exposed to too many Katharine Hepburn movies. For God's sake, turn off American Movie Channel before you grow breasts."

Pacey's going-away party is a picnic on the dock, with Grams dropping pearls of wisdom about pursuing your heart – which affects both Jen and Jack. Grams initiates a road trip to preserve teen love and Jen's ardor impresses a crowd of football jocks and a lovelorn Henry. Mission accomplished, eyes turn to resuscitate Jack's love life. His public kiss with Ethan is not well received by Brad, Ethan's boyfriend. But at least Jack has friends and family to offer him comfort and support.

At the rehearsal dinner, Joey drops a bombshell to Dawson: if she had not been forced to choose between Dawson's friendship and Pacey "... if I thought there was a chance you would forgive me, I might have chosen differently." Joey and Pacey's next meeting is near her wall on which he's now painted "Ask Me To Stay". He leaves her pensive.

At the wedding, Mitch and Gale impress everyone with the beauty of their wedding vows. Love is in the air but there is little love lost between Joey and Dawson – especially when Pacey turns up. The boys exchange harsh words with Pacey rhetorically asking, "Things will never be the same between us, will they?" Dawson's wedding speech touches on recognizing that love is the ability to always forgive. Privately, he tells Joey to seek Pacey.

"I could live with myself if you chose Pacey instead of me, I couldn't if you didn't choose Pacey because of me." He sets Joey free, but the action has its price for both of them. Andie, Jen, and Jack refuse to let Dawson sink.

Back home, Jack angrily relates his problems to his father: "I didn't ask to be gay," and is crumbling when his dad stuns him by saying how Jack's taught him to love because of someone's differences. They share a hug that's been long in coming.

Joey tells Pacey that the whole year had been about people trying to stop others from moving on, growing up. She finally admits "I think I'm in love with you," then madly hops aboard to sail away with her love – with just the clothes she stands up in!

Episode Music

Sinead O'Connor – 'Jealous'
Jann Arden – 'Sleepless'
Jessica Andrews – 'Riverside'
Pancho's Lament – 'Promise Me This'
Janis Ian – 'Days Like These'
Better Days – 'Walking In My Sleep'
Jessica Andrews – 'I Will Be There For You'

Season IV
Coming Home . . . . Episode #401
Written by Greg Berlanti
Directed by Greg Prange
Not exactly a hero's welcome for the complicated couple.

Joey to Jen
(about Pacey): "We did it. All day, all night. Twenty-four seven. Were you aware that there are at least thirty-eight known differing sexual positions? And forty-two if you're flexible enough."

After a whole summer together and Pacey and Joey are still loved up, even contemplating not returning to Capeside and living the life of pirates. On their return, they have a lot to catch up on but Pacey warns Joey to be prepared for people asking the crass – but interesting – question whether they did it or not. Dawson discovers Pacey's sister Gretchen (whom he had a crush on) is back in town. Pacey also discovers, and notes with dismay, that she has usurped his place at Doug's apartment.

When Joey doesn't dish the dirt, Bessie reveals how well the business has been doing – so well that Joey's got to spend a few days on the couch! While visiting the empty Leery house, Joey notices "her" ladder has gone and Dawson's now into photography. Jen fills her in on the news: how she and Henry now have a long-distance relationship as he took up a boarding

school scholarship. Jen's the second to ask The Question but Joey's not saying. She accepts Jen's invitation to a movie and then invites a hesitant Pacey. At the open-air movie, the mood's tense and as the couple head towards the gang, Pacey takes a moment to talk privately with Gretchen, who's not surprised he's hooked up with Joey. She is more reticent about why she's left college though.

Dawson and Joey play a game of "I'm not coming over first" that is blatantly apparent to everyone. Dawson eventually meets and greets but conversation's stale and painful. When Pacey returns, he grabs Joey under the illusion she's ready to depart. An argument ensues between the pair with Pacey claiming Dawson's all she can think about. Ironically, Pacey's departure leaves you-know-who to drop Joey home. Conversation's more well-oiled now, with Joey saying: "I'm sorry for everything that happened last year and for doing what I had to do." Her gift to him is a brick from Ernest Hemingway's home as a token to represent the foundation of a new friendship.

Andie finds the guts to introduce herself to a pair of cute French tourists who speak little or no English and gives them a wack tour of the town. At the movie, Andie continues to ramble in English, not realizing that one has tricked her into thinking he understands no English. Mortification rules... and mutual attraction. J.J's actually an American studying in Paris. They share a kiss.

Why sleep on the Potter Bed-and-Breakfast couch when you have True Love to find? Joey explains to Pacey how she needed to see Dawson as he's been a long-time friend, one who she's hurt terribly. But her heart remains with Pacey. He's convinced.

Episode Music

Everclear – 'AM Radio'
Mary Beth – 'Souvenirs'
David Gray – 'This Year's Love'

Failing Down .... Episode #402
Written by Tom Kapinos
Directed by Sandy Smolan

Senior year in high school is the one to enjoy – it should not be the one to repeat.

Dawson's not impressed to find Pacey and Joey snogging outside his registration class. Joey takes a chance to apologize to Andie who says they all used the summer "to get over ourselves" and stop treating Pacey and Joey's relationship as a cataclysm. She also hints at a job at the Capeside Yacht Club – and advises her to drop the name Ross if the interview is tough. Mrs Valentine makes said interview tough as hell but hires Joey once the name hits the air. But Owen Ross shows up, critiquing the exclusive clan. He turns out to be Drue, Mrs Valentines' son.

Pacey's new guidance counsellor, who is none other than Mitch, informs Pacey he should have been in summer school and thus has to forego working after school to do extra classes. Apartment hunting together, Pacey elaborates his problems to Gretchen, but not Joey. Dawson finds out from Mitch and though he feigns indifference, he tells Joey. She's defensive claiming she would have known if Pacey was in academic trouble. "When you love someone, you want her to be proud

Dawson to Jen:
"...feelings can change, passion will fade, partners will come and go, but through it all, one thing remains sacred: friendship."

of you," Dawson advises, and she understands. Joey's comment that Pacey always runs away from trouble quietens Pacey. Next day, Gretchen adds that it's no surprise he's a tad insecure with father and brother's deprecating comments – but feeling he's not worthy of Joey comes courtesy of Dawson comparisons. When Gretchen pays Dawson a visit, she thanks him for thinking of her stubborn younger brother and a new friendship is born.

Jen feels deserted by Henry – who ironically emails Jack to say he's seeking a break. Jack, stunned, confides in Andie who warns him to "proceed with caution". Jen's thunderous face when she finds out confirms directions were not heeded. Dawson reminds Jen of the importance of friendship, which will help her through any romantic rigmarole. She and Jack make up, with him offering a broad, friendly shoulder for her tears.

When Pacey apologizes to Joey she reminds him how they're forging their own history and assures him: "I'm not going anywhere without you."

Episode Music

Say-So – 'How Could We Know'
Eels – 'Packing Blankets'
Stew – 'Cavity'
Five Way Friday – 'Homecoming'
The Lads – 'Alone'
Five For Fighting – 'Superman'

Two Gentlemen of Capeside .... Episode #403
Written by Jeffrey Stepakoff
Directed by Sandy Smolan

True Love flounders while friendship prospers.

Dawson and Joey have a classroom discussion over the merits of *Two Gentlemen of Verona*, which is about a young woman coming between the friendship of two men. New boy Drue encourages the teacher, Mr Kasdan to let the pair have a debate – but teacher makes it a threesome.

To celebrate an "A", Pacey invites Joey sailing but as she's studying, Jen offers her services. On the deep blue sea, she's enjoying herself, even though there are hints of a storm.

Andie's new medication is making her queasy but she's determined to meet with Mrs Valentine to discuss a college application. Once her mental illness surfaces, Valentine gets mean: "... perhaps someone with your background would do better in a less competitive environment." Andie's not having it, stating firmly that her illness and recovery has made her a stronger person.

While studying at the Capeside Yacht Club, Drue compares Dawson, Pacey, and Joey to the *Star Wars* clique of Luke Skywalker, Han Solo, and Princess Leia. Joey and Dawson are not amused. The discussion about the play incites Dawson to exclaim: "Pacey and I are not going to be friends again." He feels that while Joey has apologized, Pacey shows no remorse. Customer Arthur Brooks warns Joey about a storm and it soon starts getting breezy.

Out at sea, things are decidedly choppy as the electrics on *True Love* short out and the boat is battered by waves. There's little chance of making it back to the harbor, so Pacey heads for a sheltered cove. Though there's no form of communication available, he hopes against hope that Dawson will remember the spot the pair used as kids. On land, Joey alerts everyone to Pacey and Jen being in danger. Dawson immediately remembers the cove and as he heads out in Brooks' boat, Joey declares she needs to go to prevent her worrying about both Dawson and Pacey.

Drue to Dawson and Joey:
"You're obviously Luke to that Pacey guy's Han Solo. You're the stuff of pre-teen daydreams. Cute, smart – non-threatening. Which is great and all but not for Princess Joey here, who's clearly smack dab in the middle of her bad boy phase."

Joey:
"And where do you fit into this scenario, Drue? Jabba the Hutt, maybe?"

Andie's skill under the swirling pressure of the storm is inversely mirrored by Mrs Valentine turning to jelly. At sea, Jen's terrified and encourages Pacey to speak up on any regrets he may have. Eventually, Pacey divulges that he's upset at the current situation with Dawson. Not too long after, the brave devil himself arrives. They lash the boats together and Jen jumps across. Time for Pacey and, whoops, he cannot leave *True Love*! Incredibly, Dawson jumps across shouting, "I'm not leaving you!" and drags Pacey to safety.

Everyone's pleased at the gang's safe return – with Dawson hailed a hero. Andie gets an opportunity to cut Mrs Valentine down to size and leaves with her pride intact. Joey's mad at Pacey and pleased he's safe but she also warns him to acknowledge his friendship with Dawson. Inside the Capeside Yacht Club Jen bumps into Drue – a decidedly unwelcome acquaintance from New York.

Episode Music

Jayhawks – 'I'm Gonna Make You Love Me'

Shawn Colvin – 'Never Saw Blue Like That'

Pacey looks for Dawson the next day to offer his sincere thanks and to add his apology: "I'm sorry because I miss our friendship. And however far off it may be, I look forward to the day that we can be friends again."

Future Tense .... Episode #404
Written by Gina Fattore
Directed by Michael Lange

And where do you see yourself in five years' time?

The specter of college applications affects the Capeside crew differently. Ms Watson the college advisor says Joey could "... probably get in anywhere in the country," but Joey finds herself unable to confide in Pacey as he is "... barely going to graduate." Bessie tells her not to apologize for her dreams. When Joey reveals to Pacey her belief that doing well in school would automatically open doors now appears a tad naïve – he reminds her how many people would love her problems.

Dawson to Gale:

"... college isn't the be-all and end-all that parents make it out to be. Because once you get past all the rhetoric about great books no-one actually reads, it's really just this big holding pen for 18–22-year-olds. Like prison with a better meal plan."

Even while interviewing for a bartending job at Leery's Fresh Fish, Gretchen keeps the reason for leaving college to herself. Dawson's comment to Gale: "Most people aren't in college to learn. They're there to kill brain cells and commingle with the opposite sex," elicits the concerned response that Dawson may be seeking colleges miles from home just to escape Joey.

Drue irks Jen the way she feared. She warns him: "The kind of fun we had, Drue – I don't have anymore." This warning doesn't prevent one of Jen's New York indiscretions from throwing her a birthday party – which Jen's duty bound to attend to avoid being labelled stuck up. She works out it is somebody else's summerhouse and should the cops arrive, all everyone will remember is her name!

Dawson notices Joey drinking – and is not happy. He wonders aloud why she, who is about to reap hard-worked-for rewards, wants to drown herself in alcohol. But she is unable to reason sensibly with him. She gives Jen pause for thought as she slurs how Mr Valentine abandoned Drue and his mom to poverty. Jen

apologizes to Drue for being harsh but he proves he's still a jerk by presenting her with Ecstasy tablets. She declines but Drue leaves them there with a wink.

At football, Jack injures his shoulder which Andie sees as a sign to allow him time to do college applications. Jack does not, snapping: "I'm happy for you that everything's going so well... but I don't need you to control my life." When she apologizes later, he says gently: "You have to let me make my own mistakes."

Dropping Joey home, Pacey understands her fears were about leaving him behind. He states: "I don't plan to be here. I plan to be wherever you are."

Late that night, at Leery's Fresh Fish, Dawson finds Gretchen. For every quarter she bounces into a glass, he has to open his heart and reveal a secret. Damn, she's good at bouncing. He spills that he knows how much Joey loves Pacey. "I've seen it on her face. I've seen them hold hands. And tonight I saw them fighting." Gretchen's wisdom likens life to *The Wizard of Oz*. How can the best line be "There's no place like home" when the journey is Technicolor and filled with great friends, while real life is dull and black and white.

Episode Music

Moxie Starpark – 'Sorry'
Mike Plume – 'Something To Say'
Filibuster – 'Backstreets'
Supreme Beings of Leisure – 'Never The Same'
Crushing Velvet – 'Sugar Star'
Medium – 'Five Alive'
Julie Plug – 'Please, Please'
Lori Carson – 'You Won't Fall'
Train – 'Respect'
Wild Colonials – 'Day Ditty'
Katie Reider – 'What You Don't Know'

A Family Way .... Episode # 405
Written by Maggie Friedman
Directed by Nancy Malone

Dawson's only-child status is threatened.

Leery's Fresh Fish is doing fine but Gale looks a little peaky. It's Gretchen who tells Dawson and Mitch she may well be pregnant. A home test reveals Gale is with child and while Mitch is ecstatic, Dawson and Gale are a little more reserved. Gale later breaks Mitch's heart by saying she's contemplating a termination as there are so many negatives in having a baby at the moment.

Dawson acknowledges to Gretchen that he feels his parents are irresponsible. She reminds him to spare a thought for his mom, 40, pregnant, little money, renewed relationship. The subject makes Gretchen uncomfortable. Dawson's distraught at the prospect of abortion but Gale yells she's not ready to "... handle the mistakes" of motherhood again. Gretchen later recalls her own experience of falling pregnant, deciding to get an abortion but then miscarrying. The guilt remained with her though. Dawson levels problems with his mom by reminding her "You're not afraid to make mistakes, and to pick up and keep going and try new things." Gale and Mitch are intensely grateful to a son sensitive enough to put their feelings first.

Andie has roped Jack into coaching junior high soccer. A lil' girl with attitude, called Molly, promises to give trouble, though not equal to the amount her man-hungry sister, Caroline, gives. Despite Jack wisely telling Andie: "Gay is kind of a controversial word when you're talking about working with kids," he ends up blurting to Caroline who, humiliated, tells the parents on the team. Some remove their kids, claiming Jack's "dangerous". He's deeply hurt and even Andie's optimism cannot dissuade him from wallowing in a dark mood.

Jack to Andie:
"I'm a good person, and people look at me and they see something awful. Do you have any idea how that feels?"

Pacey turns the tables on Joey, stopping her amorous advances. She's surprised and confides her desire for sex to Jen, but cannot explain why she is still hesitant. Jen says she needs to ensure that – ready or not – she is prepared. At Capeside's free clinic, Joey's embarrassed and shocked by a stream of questions about sexually transmitted diseases and the

consequences of pregnancy. She takes her bag of free goodies and is glad to exit. Bessie discovers the bag of condoms and various other forms of protection but says nothing – until they're at a table crowded with bed-and-breakfast guests: "You are not ready to have sex," Bessie declares. It is Bodie who reminds Joey that Bessie does not want her to make the same mistakes she did. During a make-out session with Pacey, Joey warns him about ever trying to manipulate her again by rebuffing her advances when he has ulterior motives.

Painting Mr Brooks' house to pay for denting his boat, Dawson has to put up with the old man's criticism of his photos: "These photos are cold. Unemotional." Later, Brooks is impressed, in his quiet way, with a photo of Gretchen. He says: "... you're not only shooting her melancholy, but your own."

Looking through baby photos, Gale appears to be reconsidering her earlier decision.

Episode Music

Five Way Friday – 'Everyone'
Pete Yorn – 'Just Another'
Bright Blue Gorilla – 'Feel The Movement'
Verbow – 'Crest of Mary'

Great Xpectations .... Episode #406
Written by Nan Hagan
Directed by Bruce Seth Green

Drue's bad influence begins to affect even the most strait-laced.

At the local record store, Gretchen finds out about a rave and tells Dawson how "every generation has its rebel sub-culture experience." It transpires Gretchen has given the speech to everyone, though Pacey and Joey are surprised when Dawson shows. Gretchen warns them to be careful at the party. Though the tension's palpable between Dawson and Pacey, the warmth Gretchen oozes to Dawson is noticeable as well.

The rave gives Drue an excuse – not that he needed one – to continue bothering Jen. He claims the drugs he had left at the party went missing and says: "If you're gonna take one, tonight's the perfect night."

Andie continues to offer advice on college applications to the Capeside gang – but it seems she's the one to listen to as she wins a spot at Harvard. But Andie's not as elated as everyone else. The party offers an excuse to chill out for a while. Getting ready at Jen's, she catches her with the Ecstasy tabs and is awfully curious. Jen reveals how she was on Ecstasy when she lost her virginity. Andie pops a pill, much to Jen's shock and worry.

Dawson to Joey:
"Used to be parties were bowling and birthday cakes. Now they're high-risk ventures that could actually kill. Another perk of growing up in the millennium."

Drue, Joey, Pacey, Gretchen, Dawson, Jack, Jen, and Andie are washed with music and lights. First chance she gets, Joey asks Gretchen if there's anything occurring between her and Dawson. Gretchen replies no, but promptly checks with Dawson to ensure there are no crossed wires. Dawson reassures her he is only seeking friendship.

Andie's kite-high, overcome with the lights, the music, the love she thinks she feels from the beautiful people in the room. Jen's the only one who notices – until Drue cottons on and whisks Andie away from protective eyes. Outside,

Andie spots Pacey and Joey and confesses: "... Pace, you are the love of my life. I'm so not over you." A little later, her trip starts to turn bad and she collapses into convulsions, worrying the hell out of everyone. Jack's stunned when, in the medic area, he says she's on an anti-depressant – only for Jen to add that she's also dropped Ecstasy. The combination is dangerous and Andie's taken to hospital with a furious Jack yelling to Jen: "That should be you in that ambulance." At the hospital, Pacey feels guilty that he didn't recognize the signs and stays while everyone else goes home.

At Grams' house, Jen's guilt mounts. She blames herself for Abby Morgan's death (Episode # 218, *A Perfect Wedding*, Abby drowns while out drinking with Jen). Drue reckons what is really sinful is the way the gang reacted: "Monday, at school, they'll treat you like this is your fault." He tries to side with Jen but she sees the subterfuge and requests his departure.

Episode Music

Poe – 'Hey Pretty'
Stephen Boyd – 'So In Love'
Granian – 'Far From Saved'
Chemical Brothers – 'Block Rockin'
Beats'
Chemical Brothers – 'Setting Sun'
Chemical Brothers – 'Leave Home'
Symbiosis – 'Protocol'
Eva Cassidy – 'Fields of Gold'

Andie apologizes to her father but he is not mad – unlike Jack, who warns that their family has been through enough without an additional blow.

Dawson and Joey have breakfast together and ruminate on how parties used to be about bowling but now they can be dangerous affairs. They also contemplate the departure for college, with Joey saying: "I think about it sometimes and wherever we go next... it's kinda hard to imagine life without you." Dawson tells her not to get rid of her rowing boat just yet as there will be a nipper at the Leery house to keep Alexander company. Mitch and Gale have decided to keep the baby.

You Had Me At Goodbye .... Episode #407
Written by Chris Levinson & Zack Estrin
Directed by John Behring

The blame game reaches a climax as the Capeside crew ponder how well they know each other.

Joey requires a peer recommendation from "The Person Who Knows You Best" for a college application. Ouch. Gretchen, surprisingly, insists Joey be "selfish" and ask Dawson. His response: "Are you sure I'm the right person to do this?" doesn't instil confidence in her.

Brooks is insistent that Dawson complete working off his debt for the boat – even though Dawson has college applications to work on. Brooks later observes that Dawson does not face his "issues". He warns it's possible to lose people from your life through no mistake of your own. The minute Dawson starts deconstructing though, Brooks jumps up stating "Gonna monologue me to death, I can feel it coming ..." Dawson returns to Joey with her recommendation unwritten. Pacey, overhearing the exchange, wades in once Dawson's left. "It's not that you asked Dawson, it's the question, Joey. 'Person Who Knows You Best.' When do I get to be that person?"

Arthur Brooks to Dawson:
"Teenage angst gives me heartburn."

Drue claims he has always been there for Jen but she insists she will never look to him for solace, despite her friends not speaking to her. Drue later squeals to Mitch (in school counselor role) about the Ecstacy tablets and he and Jen are sentenced to 100 hours community service. More hurtful though is Grams' intensity: "I have never been more purely and utterly disappointed in anything or anyone in all my life." Jen finds her way

to the McPhee's to tell Jack that the way he's shutting her out for making a mistake is something she would never do.

Andie, meanwhile, is reluctant to go back to school fearing the gossip and expresses concern to Pacey that friendships continue to split – especially Jack and Jen's. Later, Mr McPhee tells Andie she could graduate early and chill with an aunt in Florence until Harvard beckons. Jack's not enamored with the idea. He had always pictured Andie as: "... the girl who didn't just go to the last party of senior year but threw it." At Leery's Fresh Fish, Andie calls the gang together. Jen's last to come – but before she and Jack can start, Andie announces she's leaving Capeside. It's a good thing Brooks was not present as Andie's monologue would have killed him. She relates how the gang is in tatters; how Jen is not to blame for her error; how Dawson, Pacey, and Joey have a history back to the cradle. "Time's ticking. Your lives in Capeside are almost over, do you really want them to end this way?"

The meal is long and the apologies come thicker than gravy. Pacey reflects on why he reacted from the gut about the recommendation – Joey reminds him Dawson knew her best but in years to come, it will be Pacey who knows her best. Jack says to Jen he was worried she was "changing" on him. Dawson

Episode Music

Everclear – 'Wonderful'
The Normals – 'Two Wrongs And A Right'
Michelle Cummings – 'Freedom From Shame'
Sarah McLachlan – 'I Will Remember You'

asks for another chance at the recommendation: "I may not always be the guy who knows you best, Joey. But I'm glad I knew you first." Saying goodbye to Andie , Pacey is overwhelmed. He has done this before (Episode #221, *Ch-ch-changes*, her departure due to her breakdown) and it doesn't get easier. "You know what I think we're all gonna miss most about you, McPhee? Your overwhelming optimism."

Dawson's photography skills come in mighty handy as he captures the gang, all together, for the last time. For now at least.

The Unusual Suspects .... Episode #408
Written by Jon Kasdan
Directed by James Whitmore, Jr.

A whodunit in the best of the tradition.

Monday morning and Principal Peskin's sailboat and dog, Chester, are in the school swimming pool – a prank to salute the class of 2001. The dog incriminates Jack by being extremely friendly. But there are others who need to explain themselves. Pacey has access to the boat club while Dawson has access to Mitch's master keys. In flashback mode, we get access to the previous day.

Jack's alibi? Apart from a brief visit to a hardware shop with Drue to get materials for a chemistry project, Jack spent most of the day with Jen. He informs her that her community service can be whittled down by helping him with the soccer team. She's good, helping him to win over Molly and encouraging her to play in goal. The pushy soccer dads aren't happy, threatening to fire him if they lose the game. Despite the fact they win, they still fire Jack.

Pacey's alibi? Well, with a recent career aptitude test indicating he would be

good in law enforcement, he has decided to shadow Doug for a day. First stop? Donuts. Then Pacey questions Doug about the pointlessness of his profession when he had high aspirations as a kid. Doug's not impressed: "If you ever ... presume to judge me again, I will beat the ugly out of you." Looking for Principal Peskin's dog, they have no luck and abandon the search – for now. When they later find Drue skulking around the boatyard, he insists his mother had received a call telling her a boat was missing and he is let off. Drue gives Pacey a lift home where he insists he went straight to bed. Peskin is satisfied and lets him leave. On exiting, Pacey says it's unlikely Dawson would play the prank, being the "honorable" guy that he is.

Ten-year-old Molly to Jack (about a jerk named Billy, also ten): "Just wait 'till I'm seventeen and hot. He'll regret messing with me."

Dawson's alibi? He was at Brooks' place clearing his mammoth study where he happened upon a year book which showed that the young Brooks had wanted to be a movie director. But when Dawson's and Pacey's oath to do a stunning Senior prank is discovered, things are looking shaky. Back at the Leery's, Drue is waiting to return Mitch's keys which Dawson had left in his new chum's car. Brooks and Dawson later get into it, with Brooks shocking the young boy with a fearsome tongue-lashing. Despite this, Dawson returns insisting he cannot be dismissed that easily. As he is released, Dawson sticks up for Pacey saying "he's not an idiot" and would not have done the prank.

When Peskin accuses Drue, Mrs Valentine is not full of love. "You gentlemen should be ashamed." Peskin outlines how Drue did it, buying paint in the hardware shop; copying Mitch's keys; lurking at the boat shed. Drue's smile is enigmatic, but perhaps not for the reason Peskin suspects. On exiting the school, Drue says to Joey: "Karma finally caught up with me."

After the long day of interrogation, Caroline brings a red-eyed Molly to Jack. He explains that his job loss was not her fault and people often do things because "... they're afraid of things they don't understand." Doug says it's unlikely Pacey will make a good lawman. "You were born to break the rules, not enforce them." Using the internet, Dawson discovers that Brooks actually had a successful film career.

When Joey confronts Dawson, Pacey, and Jack, they cannot help but admit their scam – in a highly hypothetical way of course. Burying incriminating evidence, Pacey says to Dawson: "Do you think it's possible that maybe, I could prove to you that I could be someone you could trust again, someday?" Dawson finds the supposition acceptable.

Episode Music
Evan & Jaron – 'Crazy For The Girl'
Dar Williams – 'After All'

Kiss Kiss Bang Bang . . . . Episode #409
Written by Tom Kapinos
Directed by Perry Lang

Has Brooks never heard the song that says something about Christmas being the season to be jolly?

Movie Night is reborn with Gretchen and Dawson watching one of Brooks' flicks. Dawson is stunned, Gretchen unimpressed. When Dawson enthuses to Brooks, the old man remains nonchalant. College advisor Ms Watson recommends Dawson redo his "Why Do You Want To Be A Filmmaker?" essay as he stylishly skirts the question. Attempting to use Brooks as a resource, Dawson admits how he simply stopped making films. "... life got in the way. And my heart wasn't in it anymore."

Mrs Valentine continues her mean ways to Joey, making snide remarks about Bessie and Bodie. She warms up though when Mr Kubelik turns up, a rep from Worthington University who plans to host a networking party. Joey later expresses concern to Gretchen about taking Pacey: "I'm just worried he's gonna feel out of place." He's incredibly reluctant but, of course, turns up, having scrubbed up real good. Dinner is a little stilted until Pacey starts to win the crowd over with his warmth and humor. He is especially charming with Mr Kubelik who even asks: "Why is it you haven't applied?" When Pacey lies how he's a Yale lad, Joey's brow furrows with anger. But it transpires that Pacey can do nothing but sing her praises – and Kubelik says its a "rare gift" to have someone like that in your life. Joey pauses for thought and expresses her heartfelt thanks to Pacey. They make their way over to the Leerys.

Dawson to Brooks:
"I guess whatever happened to you out there turned you into the kind of person who'd tear into a teenage kid whose only mistake was equating talent with kindness and wisdom."

Gretchen talks the Leerys into having a Leery Christmas party. Brooks' distemper relents and he finds his way to the party to confide to Dawson how his best friend stole his girlfriend way back in 1956 and how

he has never recovered. The pain was such that he lost the zest for movies altogether. He rekindles Dawson's enthusiasm with this tale and a newly excited Dawson says his next movie is going to be about... Arthur Brooks!

The few words Grams exchanges with Jen following the Ecstasy incident are bitter ones. The old lady doesn't bat an eyelid when Jack expresses his worry that Jen's not completed her college applications. But when Grams approaches Jen, the young lady spits: "You don't get to discuss my future with me. You lost that right when you wrote me off." With Jack though, Grams plans to coerce her granddaughter. In the middle of the Leery party, Ms Watson congratulates a confused Jen on completing her essays. Flabbergasted, Jen takes her nails out for Jack: "Did I not ask you to mind your own business?" But Grams jumps in and assures Jen she need not ask her parents for the money, she will pay for it herself. A cool interlude with fiery Brooks and fiery Grams suggests the couple have more in common than their age.

Brooks points to the mistletoe that Dawson and Gretchen happen to be standing under, and says to the shocked Leery lad: "Quit flirting and kiss her already." Gretchen makes the move and they share a beautiful kiss, then part. But Dawson wants a bit more so he leans in for another and the pair are so far gone they do not notice Joey and Pacey staring in disbelief.

Episode Music

Library – 'Nightmares'
Hathaway – 'Sorry Charlie'
Wheatus – 'Teenage Dirtbag'
Katie Reider – 'Piece of Soul'
Say-So – 'Souvenirs'
Mark Shane – 'Jingle Bells'
Franz-Joseph Haydn – 'String Quartet in C Major – Emperor'
Vikki Carr – 'The Christmas Song'
Franz-Josef Haydn – 'String Quartet No. 15'
Adam Fields – 'The First Noel'
Sue Medley – 'O Holy Night'
Shawn Colvin – 'Love Came Down At Christmas'
Smashing Pumpkins – 'Christmastime'
Mary Beth – 'Have Yourself A Merry Little Christmas'

Self Reliance .... Episode #410
Written by Gina Fattore
Directed by David Petrarca

The kiss lingers and lingers and lingers and lingers, like Christmas turkey.

Dawson and Gretchen insist The Kiss meant nothing, though to some it would seem they doth protest too much. Brooks feigns indifference to Dawson's documentary but he jumps – somewhat arthritically – at the chance to relive his glory days. He has a theory on love triangles: "... every piece of happiness ... involves somebody else's unhappiness." At a later interview session, Dawson finds that Brooks is a little clouded memory-wise. He discovers from a nurse that Brooks is unwell and failing to take his medication. For now, Dawson wonders why he wants to pursue the project.

With Bessie and Bodie out of town, Pacey helps Joey look after Alexander and the empty bed-and-breakfast. But after she kicks him out for disturbing her studies, a family of four arrive, meaning she is unprepared for a test the next day.

> *Dawson to Jack:*
> "Not every kiss has to be a completely life-changing experience, you know."

Joey had told Pacey that The Kiss did not bother her but even Gretchen acknowledges privately to Pacey that that's a "big lie." Joey insists loudly she is not bothered but of course, she is. Every time she is with Dawson, she is 15 and alone again, whereas she has matured with Pacey. He tells her she needs to confront Dawson and release her pent-up emotions. The 'confrontation' is actually pleasant, with Dawson reassuring Joey about the test and giving her a beautiful picture for a present. She responds by encouraging him to follow his heart where Gretchen is concerned.

Pacey seeks Mr Kasdan to request Joey take the test again, which he allows, reminding Joey why she is so lucky to have someone like Pacey in her corner.

Jen takes Jack to a Gay-Straight Teen coalition. Effervescent leader Tobey introduces himself and recognizes Jack from the TV story Dawson did about him. He embarrasses Jack by saying he should "confront prejudice head-on" and not roll over quietly as he feels Jack did when the soccer parents fired him. The coalition plans to challenge a bowling alley for prejudiced attitudes. At the alley, Jack reckons Tobey disapproves of him as he is not "gay enough" and departs. The coalition opts to keep Jen but not Jack – who is not at all upset.

Dawson seeks Gretchen to admit his affection. "That kiss meant more to me than just Happy Holidays." Gretchen does not requite. That said, it seems as if Dawson is still content to have unburdened himself and admitted he is taking the first steps towards getting over Joey and Pacey.

Episode Music

Beth Orton – 'Don't Need a Reason'

The Tao of Dawson .... Episode #411
Written by Jeffrey Stepakoff
Directed by Keith Samples

A simple litmus test to discover if someone had feelings for another would be a handy commodity in Capeside.

Dawson and Pacey hang together for the first time in a long time. Dawson bravely, foolishly admits to being "crazy" about Gretchen and suspects she may feel the same. Pacey is thrown and says: "Sisters are like mothers. Only pretty." Love seems to indeed be in the air as Dawson discovers Brooks and Grams are dating. Dawson expresses his concern to Jack. "I think she could get her heart broken... Brooks is dying." After her husband passing away, Jack warns that she needs to know. It transpires Grams does, but she relishes the time they have. "A single moment of true joy is powerful enough to supersede a

lifetime of sorrow." When Brooks asks Dawson's advice on a gift for Grams, Dawson reveals the depth of his concern for the pair.

Gretchen and Pacey are on a road trip to collect her car from the ex-boyfriend, Nick. On arrival though, they note it is on blocks. But

Drue to Joey:

"I absolutely did not peek down your shirt at your taupe 34C Maidenform wire-rim bra with the little pink bow on the front clasp."

Nick charms Gretchen into staying overnight and the party animal wins Pacey over immediately. So much so in fact, that Pacey hints to Nick he should try and win her heart again. While the house party rocks, a young lady gives Pacey the eye. Even though Pacey tells Nick about Joey back home, he still gives the young hombre the key to his room and informs him where the condoms are to be found. This wakes Pacey up and he seeks Gretchen to say "... he's a world-class jerk." Gretchen already knew this, of course, and divulges her pregnancy and the fact that Nick never found out. What surprises Pacey more is that Gretchen is entertaining Nick's overtures, even going upstairs with the drunken romancer. There, she realizes that closure has finally come and rescued her.

Drue has to visit his father in New York – much to his vexation. He accidentally gets himself and Joey trapped in the Yacht Club's storage room – and there's little chance of rescue until Monday morning. Joey, seeking food, has a fall and is caught by Drue who promptly kisses her – she promptly pops him one. It's only when she regrets the bruiser she has given the opportunist, that they start to connect; he divulges feelings about his absent father. Drue wonders how Pacey and Joey stay together considering they're so different. She replies that it's the differences that keep the spark alive. The day limps by and Joey and Drue are still closeted. Imagine Joey's fury when she discovers Drue had a phone. Her fury evaporates though when she realizes he orchestrated the whole thing so he would not have to spend the weekend with his father.

Episode Music

Michal – 'Broken Boy'
Nine Days – 'If I Am'
The Lads – 'Understand'
Red Delicious – 'Want Me'
Switchfoot – 'Love Is The Movement'
Red Delicious – 'Siren'
Red Delicious – 'Nocturne'
Splendor – 'I Think God Can Explain'

Jack offers Dawson decent counsel on his dilemma with Gretchen. They're decorating a spare room of the Leery house, making a nursery, when Dawson finds a letter he wrote years ago to Gretchen. Jack answers Dawson's indecision with: "... maybe this is exactly where you are supposed to be at this moment in time. With a girl you wanted way before Joey Potter." Dawson does indeed give Gretchen the letter and she runs to him, crying and overjoyed.

The Te of Pacey .... Episode #412
Written by Maggie Friedman
Directed by Harry Winer

Pacey's birthday curse and the curse of Egyptian Mummies – fact or fiction?

Pacey warns an enthusiastic Joey that his birthdays are invariably traumatic. He recalls various Pacey days, including his 16th when no one came to his party (see Episode #202, *Crossroads*). While Gretchen and Joey conspiratorially plan his surprise birthday party, Pacey receives a letter that unnerves him.

The fact that neither Dawson nor Gretchen have told Pacey and Joey they're dating suggests it's more worrisome than they will admit. When Gretchen informs Dawson she would rather wait until after the party to go on their date, he's displeased: "... if this is something we have to hide, then maybe we shouldn't be doing it in the first place."

Grams is dreamily smitten with Brooks, not even hearing Jen whinge about her last few hours of community service, driving drunken high school kids home. By coincidence, her partner will be Tobey, who has volunteered his services. He is over the moon about a fabulous new boyfriend and describes him a little too vividly. A young girl they collect reminds Jen of herself a few years ago. When Jen attempts to make the girl wise up, she simply slams out of the vehicle. Tobey commiserates with Jen for failing to educate the "... little eighth-grade Lolita". Jen, in turn recognizes that Tobey's boyfriend is pure fiction, invented to cover his affection for Jack. Jen advises him that if wants to be part of Jack's life, he should try being friendly and pleasant – a novel concept.

Pacey to Joey: "You've got the mind of a pessimist and the heart of an incurably optimistic romantic. It's quite an attractive combination."

Joey brings a blindfolded Pacey to his parent's house, where the party is to be held, but the affair is decidedly lacklustre. Pacey's back in the midst of possibly the most dysfunctional family in Capeside. They do not even pretend to make an effort for the Birthday Boy, who privately expresses his annoyance at Joey. It's obvious there's something else on his mind. When his parents start discussing his further education plans however, Pacey exits to the basement with Joey – where they discover Gretchen and Dawson entwined in a heavy, heavy make-out session.

Dawson and Gretchen try to get Pacey and Joey to discuss their relationship, but neither are interested. Once the attempt at warm family recollections turns into painful memories, Pacey is overcome: "No one is there for Pacey. No one gives Pacey a break. Everyone expects the worst of Pacey."

He then reveals that the only college he thought would accept him has actually rejected him. He exits suddenly, and Dawson and Joey pursue, giving them a chance to speak. Joey advises Dawson on the things to expect from dating a Witter: "In relationships, they tend to keep their emotions close, and their weaknesses even closer. But Dawson, it isn't because they don't care. It's because they care so much."

Ironically, it is Pacey's dad who finds him, sitting near the empty slot that used to house *True Love*. Dad relates how he never made it into the police academy the first time but had to work his cotton socks off to achieve his dream.

Gretchen admits to Dawson she's worried that a relationship with him might be interrupted by her departure from Capeside. Dawson has matured as he recognizes that people must leave at some stage – after all, he will be off to college soon.

Pacey despondently says to Joey: "We're on separate roads, moving further away from each other." Joey, however, is not so downhearted. She reassures him that despite the upcoming changes to their lives, their relationship will remain a constant.

Episode Music

Ella Fitzgerald – 'Night & Day'
Arlibido – 'Jello'
6X – 'Rock Out'
Sweetsalt – 'Camelot'
Tammy Raybould – 'Loving You'
Beth Orton – 'Lean On Me'

Hopeless .... Episode #413

Written by Nan Hagan
Directed by Krishna Rao

Double dates and meeting a new partner's friends are oft difficult progressions – for Capeside's youth, such things are torturous.

Gretchen feels Dawson's ready to meet her friends. As Brooks deteriorates, he asks Dawson to sign papers allowing him to collect the dying man's presciption drugs. After Leery departs, we note Brooks isn't even taking his medication. There's a finality to the way Dawson and Brooks finish work on the film. "The picture's not half-bad," Brooks says, revealing a pleasant side, "And not just because it's about me." Later though, Grams finds his hoard of pills but once she starts remonstrating, he replies he wants to end his life with dignity. The tears roll down Grams' cheek – she understands.

Keira and Jessica, Gretchen's friends, are present when Gale suddenly gives Dawson something he's never had before – a curfew. Privately, Dawson warns her he no longer requires parental advice from her. Ouch. The raucous sexual banter from the ladies reveals much to delicate Dawson – including how many sexual partners Gretchen has had. His eyebrows raise. When the ladies request they go on to another bar, rather than retire with Dawson, Gretchen sends him home with her car. Back home, Dawson confides to Gale she may have been right about her older woman fears. Gale offers good advice: "...remember, all her experiences make her the person that she is." With impeccable timing, Gretchen turns up, having only stayed to hear her friends' praise for Dawson. Their relationship progresses as they clarify important issues.

Drue to Anna:

"... unlike your nose job or breasts, I can't be bought."

Senior trip requires Joey to request Friday and Saturday night off. Mrs Valentine is prepared to trade if Joey and Pacey double-date with Drue and the well-to-do Anna – and ensure she has a good time. When Pacey grabs a goggle at the stunning Anna, it seems as if that doesn't sound so hard after all. Drue livens things up by saying to Joey: "... there's your perfect boyfriend draping himself all over the human equivalent of a Barbie doll, and you're as cool as a cucumber." If the Barbie had brains, it would be interesting, but she doesn't and Drue doesn't hesitate to point this out. Anna walks off, loudly ruing the day she slept with Drue!

Pacey bolsters Anna's esteem by assuring her that her skill to win men over rests upon more than her good looks. Joey deconstructs Drue skilfully: "This whole witty Drue routine you do, it's just a front for some really scared kid that's desperate for people to love him." Drue has a moment of honesty and admits he's actually no good with women, either picking on them or attempting to seduce them. He later makes an effort, apologizing to Anna, revealing a warmer side of his personality.

Tobey encourages Jack to volunteer in a kid's reading programme with him. Jack's very good, impressing Tobey with his small-people skills. After class, Tobey admits to feelings for Jack, who has to stress that there will never be anything between them as they lack the "spark" of attraction. Tobey's heartbroken.

Pacey and Joey ponder their own problems after discussing Drue and Anna. While Pacey has been glad not to sleep with Joey too soon, he's now anxious. "Eight months and counting. And I want you ... to know that if this relationship isn't progressing to the next level... it's not because of me." Joey admits she wants to... but is frightened.

Next morning, Dawson discovers Brooks – unconscious.

Episode Music

Louis Armstrong – 'What A Wonderful World'

Dionne Farris – 'Hopeless'

John Lardieri – 'Firecracker'

Flying Cordovas – 'Give You The World'

Mary Beth – 'Waiting For A Sign'

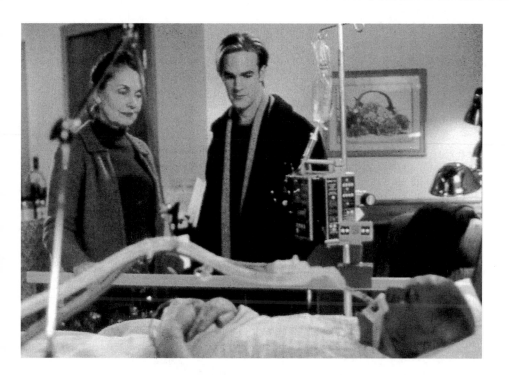

A Winter's Tale .... Episode #414

Written by Zack Estrin & Chris Levinson

Directed by Greg Prange

Snow, seduction, sex, secrets, and soul-searching occupy the gang.

While everyone else heads off on the senior trip, Dawson is staying behind with Brooks. His overdose has induced a coma and it's the machinery keeping him alive. Dawson's shocked to discover the documentation he signed now confers the right to disconnect the life-support system. Mitch and Gale are united in feeling Dawson is too young to make such a decision. It is Grams who knows that Arthur did not want to live as he was, "... let alone the way he is now."

Gretchen reassures Dawson that Brooks trusted his judgement enough to hand him a decision like this. "I think he saw how old your heart is and knew that whatever choice you made, it would be the right one." The man to whom Brooks lost the love of his life pays a visit and tells Dawson to have faith in Brooks' judgement.

Though Jack warns of the "long tradition of irresponsible sex" on trips such as this, it's unlikely the coolness that has suddenly arisen between Pacey and Joey will lead to anything more than tears. Drue has smuggled Anna aboard in the place of someone else, hoping he can sneak past the radar of Mr Kasdan. Though the rooms are supposed to be single sex, Drue distributes them to couples.

> ### Jack to Joey:
> "You came to the right place. Being Capeside's official platonic friend, women's sexual neuroses happen to be a subject with which I have some authority."

Jen sprains her ankle and though Jack promises to help her, he hadn't counted on helping her undress. In their own room, Pacey and Joey acknowledge the ice between them. They try to promise each other this weekend will not be about sex. But with Drue present, the subject inevitably erects itself over a crowded dinner. Naïve Joey reckons not all boys carry condoms in their wallets, but the ever-ready guys prove her wrong. Pacey claims to have forgotten his wallet – but Joey knows he's lying and discovers a condom in it.

Jack, claiming to feel numb – and not because of the snow – wants to do something "reckless and stupid" and with Jen, gets smashed. He professes a love more than friendship for her... and they kiss. Things get heated until Jen stops, saying: "You're drunk and you're lonely and you're gay." Stepping out of the room for iced water, she's rumbled by Kasdan.

To Jack, Joey confides: "I have so much conviction about waiting 'til the right moment." But everywhere she turns, she's challenged. And Anna's liking for Pacey is challengingly transparent. "She's what you want right?" tests Drue. Pacey replies that Joey has dragged Dawson away with them. He fears Joey has a part of her "that always thought Dawson would be your first." He leaves Joey in tears. She phones Dawson to discuss Brooks but the conversation resonates on a deeper level for them both. Dawson opts to turn the machines off, and later pays tribute to Brooks' work by showing one of his pictures to a small audience.

Drue tells Joey to beware of Anna. The towel-clad girl, meanwhile makes a pass at Pacey, only for him to respond: "It's not about wanting sex, Anna, it's about wanting to share the most intimate possible thing with someone. Even if that means waiting forever." He spins round, to find Joey had heard everything. Back in their room... she's ready.

Episode Music

Brian Charles – 'Impossible'
Epstein's Mother – 'Hideaway'
The Splytz – 'Do It Again'
Revelation Darling – 'Sucker For The Count'
Bryan Adams – 'Summer of 69'
Brian Charles – 'Dumb Love'
Crushing Velvet – 'Sugar Star'
Radford – 'How Does It Feel'
Tuck & Patti – 'Takes My Breath Away'

Four Stories . . . . Episode #415
Written by Tom Kapinos
Directed David Petrarca

Brooks' departure heralds a difficult time.

On the bus heading to Capeside, Drue tricks Kasdan into believing Pacey and Joey are already on the bus – but they're not and it departs *sans* the love couple.

Pacey and Joey's post-coital chat is witty as ever and he says "the sweetness and the sarcasm" could occupy him for the rest of his life. But, he wants to know how it was for her and the adjective "nice" is not what his "fragile male ego" requires. Joey has to remind him that she also ponders on how she measured up – after all, he has had two sexual relationships. Pacey replies that she was "... every glowing adjective under the sun." That said though, she does not want anyone to know – especially Dawson. Pacey cares not – he simply wants to do the do with the girl he loves. But, curiosity makes him wonder aloud that if Dawson were to ask – would she answer? She claims she would. Pacey then unintentionally upsets her by asking why she's failed to even touch him

all morning. Joey manages to explain how "nice" was coupled with "safe", an important word for this first-timer.

After the funeral, Grams invites Dawson to take a memento from Brooks' prop collection – which Dawson finds "completely morbid". Grams tells him that "closure does wonders for the grieving process." Dawson and Gretchen read parts from a play Brooks wrote when he was just Dawson's age. While Dawson thinks it's pathetic that only five people turned up for the funeral, Gretchen reminds him that Brooks was a guy who "saw his wildest dreams come true." What truly depresses Dawson though is the fear that what happened to Brooks – he stopped caring – could happen to any of them. Gretchen assures him it could not, Brooks actually touched Dawson's life the way Dawson has touched her life. The memento he takes? A poster. Outside, Dawson bumps into a lawyer who wants to meet with him regarding Brooks' will.

> **Pacey to Joey:**
> "I just want to be able to have sex with my girlfriend, whom I adore, and not have to worry about the soap opera repercussions of someone finding out."

On the journey back to Capeside, Jen and Jack contemplate what happened between them. Kasdan aims to give Jen the "chicken soup" she requires and she has to attend therapy with the appropriately named Tom Frost. Nervous, she spills her story adding: "I'm not sure I'm the kind of person who would benefit from therapy. I just might be too self-aware for the likes of you." When Jen gets up to leave, Frost hazards an eerily apt analysis: "...the smart, sarcastic exterior masks a scared, lonely young woman whose relationship with her parents has scarred her..." Jen sits down.

Joey and Dawson bump into each other at the movie theatre and later, Dawson tells her Brooks left him a lot of money – enough to pay his college tuition – but he's not sure what to do with it. Looking at Joey, he says something looks different. They explain how difficult it still is seeing each other with new partners, but acknowledge that there will always be deep-seated friendship and love. Just as they're departing, Dawson returns to the unshakeable feeling that something happened on the trip and asks Joey if she slept with Pacey. Her response: "I haven't slept with Pacey." And Dawson breathes a sigh of relief.

Episode Music

King Lear Jet – 'Spectre Chase'
Joseph Arthur – 'In The Sun'
Counting Crows – 'Colorblind'
Josh Rouse – 'The White Trash Period of My Life'
Bruce Patch – 'Heart & Soul'
Lisa Stansfield – 'They Can't Take That Away From Me'
Elvis Costello – 'But Not For Me'

Mind Games . . . . Episode #416

Written by Gina Fattore
Directed by David Straiton

Along with the four-letter word "love" must go that five-letter one "trust".

Frost and Jen continue their sessions, with Jen claiming she gets on better with boys as girls get "...lobotomized the second they hit puberty." After the session, Jen – together with reluctant Jack – attempt to follow Frost but bump into him. He, worldly wise, invites them to a poetry reading where Jack asks if Jen has a crush on the therapist. "He's completely not my type," a flustered Jen responds. After the reading, it transpires Frost is dating the poet. He knew all along that Jen was following him and left her knowing it was important for her to know she could trust him. And she can.

Logistics prove problematic for Pacey and Joey – the location of teenage sex has always been a trial. At school, Drue announces that Dawson and Joey have been voted Class Couple. Cue her fury but Dawson's mirth. A happy Pacey equals a sexually active Pacey. Gretchen guesses he would like the house to himself for a night. Joey's not too pleased and earliest opportunity, tells Gretchen Dawson need not know. But the older and wiser woman reminds her it's not too hard to guess. With Gale and Mitch out of town, Gretchen invites herself over to Dawson's – much to Joey and Pacey's surprise.

Dawson to Joey:

"Drue's like one of those lame TV-Batman villains – evil with a short attention span."

Dawson and Gretchen finally have their sex chat, with Dawson saying it was adult of Joey to tell him she had not consummated her relationship yet. Gretchen's face? Read confusion. She leaves. When Dawson arrives looking for Gretchen, Pacey's a little thrown. Dawson does not see Gretchen and admits that they've not had a fight but she may have "seen the light". Later, Drue will not leave Dawson to mooch in his mire and insists he and Joey will never be over one another.

Gretchen confronts Joey about her lies, wondering whether she is still confused about her choice. "... you have to tell Dawson the truth." Joey departs but before Gretchen can escape, Pacey squeezes the truth out of her about Joey's lies to Dawson. He spits: "Isn't it wonderful how the truth can just set you free?" Dawson apologizes to Joey for even asking her the sex question. Once Pacey arrives, he captures their image for the yearbook, to correct Drue's childish prank.

Episode Music

Amy Cook – 'Windows'
Josh Rouse – 'Laughter'
Low – 'In Metal'

When Gretchen speaks to Dawson it's to stress the trust aspect of the relationship. It is more difficult, she says, than sex, it's a "gigantic act of faith." It's a leap Joey has made but a little problematically. Pacey almost asks her why she lied to Dawson but opts not to – for now.

Admissions .... Episode #417
Written by Barb Siebertz
Directed by Lev L. Spiro

Lying to someone because you don't want to hurt them? Why not try telling them the truth because they deserve it?

Joey and Dawson receive college-related news. While she got into Worthington, he did not get into NYU. Bessie plans a congratulatory barbecue and while Pacey's sincerely happy, he states his worst-case scenario: joining the police and commuting to Joey on weekends.

It is to Gretchen that Dawson expresses his displeasure: "If NYU doesn't want me, USC is definitely not gonna want me, and where does that leave me?" Gretchen assures him that film school doesn't have to be the opener to his career. Jen and Jack, heading to college together, have to whittle their acceptances down. At therapy, Jen reveals her reluctance for New York – Jack's favourite. Because of her parents, Jen wants nothing to do with the city. Frost encourages

delving deep and Jen turns to Drue to recall their last night in New York. She had used Drue to get back at her father who was already disgusted with her after catching her making love to Billy. Frost speaks truth in showing Jen her acting out was solely to do with self-loathing. A breakthrough. Jack's happy but, sarcastic as ever, comments: "... it's only since you've been seeing a psychologist that I'm starting to think you may in fact be crazy."

Joey soon discovers dreams come at a price, and Worthington have decided that, because the Potter Bed-and-Breakfast is now making a profit, the Potters could afford $15,000 in tuition fees. The idea of loans is repugnant, as graduation day would also cue the start of huge repayments. Joey's devastated but opts to keep quiet and continue with the barbecue.

Though he shouldn't, Pacey confides in Gretchen that he may be a little happy Joey's not going to Worthington. In the midst of the party, Mitch and Gale bring Dawson an acceptance letter from USC. Dawson finds Joey crying and she finally admits the financial impossibilities. With little pause, Dawson offers her Brooks' money and leaves her to contemplate. She decides that the thought of accepting such a large sum is scary enough, bound to sunder their friendship.

When Dawson discusses finances with Pacey he finds him suspicious of $15,000 "with no strings attached." But once Dawson elaborates on how Joey would not be happy "anyplace else" Pacey pauses. He translates this argument to Joey, reminding her she is already indebted by all Dawson has done for her as a friend. She finds Dawson, finally confessing her lie about not sleeping with Pacey. He gives her the check saying: "... I am absolutely certain that giving you this money is the right thing to do. Because I'll always be certain of you and me, Joey. And what we mean to each other."

Jack to Jen: "Now be a good psychologically damaged child and go back to therapy and work this out."

Episode Music

Semisonic – 'Chemistry'
Marcy Playground – 'Bye Bye'
Anne McCue – 'More Than This'
Eels – 'The Sound of Fear'

Eastern Standard Time .... Episode #418
Written by Jonathan Kasdan
Directed by David Grossman

Something's rotten in the core of New York.

Dawson feels the need to escape and shoots off in the jeep with Gretchen. She fears it could change everything but Dawson is ready for that eventuality – but not a flat tyre. At a nearby town, Dawson tries to secure a replacement while Gretchen gets sandwiches.

When it becomes clear that neither Gretchen nor Dawson has the money for the tyre, the mechanic wants nothing more to do with them. Gretchen wants to hitch-hike, but Dawson instead points to a sign indicating a town within walking distance. Gretchen loves the impulsive new Dawson but reckons: "Joey having lost her virginity to Pacey makes you wonder why you weren't that guy." Dawson now realizes that often, dreams and reality conflict. He does not know what he's been waiting for. While Gretchen wants to consummate the relationship, she feels Dawson still wants to prove something, so she will bide her time.

Pacey to Drue (holding the fake ID he's just been given): "... this is a picture of a short balding Asian guy in his forties. Not my doppelganger."

In New York for Jen's visit to her prospective university, Joey's overcome by the sheer size of everything. Friends make Jen feel very welcome. Joey works out that Jen's not there for the university. She's there to see her father. Theo

Lindley is impressive and warmly welcomes Jen and Joey, booking a restaurant to celebrate Jen's university acceptance. Both Jen and Joey are overpowered by Theo's intoxicating presence and before anyone can think of confrontation, he skips out, leaving a wad of money for his daughter's entertainment in the city. Joey allows Jen to go and see her father by herself. Once there, the memories flow free and Jen relates how she caught her father making love to Annie, who was her neighbour and more like a sister. His response: "You've imagined this Jennifer," makes Jen realize that all along he had known and had allowed her to tumble into self-disgust. Forgiveness – for him and for her – is something she has taken the first steps towards.

At school, Drue invites Pacey to skip classes, but he cannot afford to. Stuck in a junior calculus class, he's in hell. At lunch, the banality of it all gets to Pacey to the point where he and Drue skip out to an ugly bar. Pacey almost begins to wax about his loneliness but opts not to – at least before the tequila takes hold. Barman Mack dislikes the pair with the phoney ID the moment they run out of money and get rowdy. When Doug arrives, Pacey finally breaks down: "This is my whole life," he cries despairingly.

At therapy, Jen feels it has now gone far enough. "I don't really have anything more to say."

Episode Music

Susan James – 'Last Lament'
Macy Gray – 'I Can't Wait To Meetchu'
Red Delicious – 'Bring You Down'
Hypnogaja – 'You Belong To Me'
Erin McKeown – 'Love In Two Parts'
Frostbit Blue – 'The Preacher'
Tricky Woo – 'Sad Eyed Woman'
John Campbelljohn – 'World Is Crazy'
Wallflowers – 'Letters From The Wasteland'
Vanessa Daou – 'Show Me'
Cowboy Junkies – 'Sweet Jane'

Late .... Episode #419
Written by Jeffrey Stepakoff
Directed by David Petrarca

Timing is all.

Tobey, struggling with his reading group, is a tad piqued at Jack's lateness. A pupil named Will also has a thing against tardiness, especially when it's his mother. Next day, Tobey fails to show. When Jack turns up at his house, he realizes he's been gay-bashed and does not want to report it to the police. To Jen, Jack says: "The paradox is that he's the guy who got up on a soap box when I first met him, and carried on about taking action." Jack returns with an officer and Tobey explains the atrocity of the attack. Ironically, Jack has also learned a lot. "We're not so different you and I, Tobey. I used to think we were – but we're not."

This week's occasion to get together? A "naming shower" for Gale's baby. She's ten months pregnant and, worryingly, there are plans, if baby doesn't come soonish, to do a Caesarean section because of Gale's age.

Gretchen's job application for *Boston Magazine* has led to an interview. Though Dawson should be happy, he's a little taken aback. It throws the reality of their upcoming separation into their faces. Joey frantically hunts for Pacey, suspecting his "fishing trip" is a cover. Gretchen tells her about Pacey's drunken adventures and how Doug has

Gale:
"Did you remember the birthing music?"
Mitch:
"I got Enya, John Tesh, Kenny G."
Gale:
"I'm having a baby, not going into a coma."

taken him camping to talk sense. "I want you to promise me that you won't do anything right now that will put additional pressure on him." Joey's answer is that her period is late. It's obvious she is unwilling to face a pregnancy test right now. The shower is a particularly difficult time for Joey. Her suggestion for a name is replaced by the necklace Dawson gave to her (see Episode #302, *Homecoming*). She leaves the room overwrought and Bessie clocks on quickly. "I can't believe it." Joey expresses her disgust with Bessie's life choices – we know how she wants to escape Capeside.

Gretchen explains to Dawson that she was unable to sleep with him as their impending separation would become more difficult. Back home, Gretchen receives a visit from Joey. She explains her experience in this area but is still able to give decent advice, telling Gretchen to cherish her time with Dawson. Instead of going for the interview, Gretchen passes her time smooching with Dawson.

After two false alarms, Gale goes into labour for real. It's a night and a day before the little girl is born. Joey's breath is taken away by the fact they have named her Lillian, after her mother.

Episode Music

Joan Baez – 'Forever Young'
Micha Green – 'Family Circus'
Karen Blake – 'Why Walk When You Can Fly'

Joey returns to apologize to Bessie: "I only hope that I have enough strength and courage to build a life for myself that's even remotely like yours." Joey finally takes the test – it's negative. When Pacey calls, she pretends she knows nothing about the real reason for his absence.

Promicide . . . . Episode #420
Written by Maggie Friedman
Directed by Jason Moore

Senior prom equals laughter, jokes, corsages and limousines...

Prom time again and Joey's a little worried about Pacey's cool attitude, and that's not cool as in cucumber.

Jen's working hard to suppress New York memories. To Joey she says: "... if I think about it I'm afraid I might... freak out or fall apart..." Instead, she occupies herself with setting up a reluctant Jack to go to the prom with Tobey.

"Why get mad when you can get even?" Jack feels and thus, Jen has to go with Drue Valentine.

Shopping for tuxes, Jack warns Dawson about after-prom sex with Gretchen: "... adding sex to the mix could serve to complicate the navigation of already difficult emotional terrain." Later Gretchen, upset, tells Dawson she did not get the Boston job – no college degree. Dawson and Joey, on their way to the prom comment on how "healthy" they are, considering the past tumultuous 12 months. The corsages Pacey bought are wilted, the limo he ordered, a rusty airport van. Cue feelings of inadequacy.

En route to the prom, Jen's keeps her spirits up with a handy supply of miniature vodka bottles in her purse. Pacey acknowledges he's a hypocrite but still asks her if that's wise. Jen knows it's not, but continues to swig. Pacey's melancholy concerns the fact that: "I don't know what the future holds. But it doesn't hold what they think it does."

The prom, set on a boat, is a dream. However, Joey can't get Pacey to confide in her. He simply says he's trying to be perfect for her – which upsets her even more. He moans: "I act gloomy, you get mad, if I act happy, you get mad..." Outside, Jen continues to drown her sorrows, leaning over the railing with a truly worried Drue supporting her. He is unswervingly attentive to her, encouraging her to move forward to college in a new city instead of returning to old New York.

Jack finally confronts his affection for Tobey: "... you were so... out, you know, and so okay with it... it put me off." But those feelings have changed, as the kiss they share reveals.

Jack to Tobey: "...How many times do I have to tell you that this is strictly platonic before you'll believe me?"

Gretchen is not enjoying the prom; after all, she did graduate four years ago. She laments to Pacey: "My life is going nowhere, I don't know what I'm gonna do... I never felt pathetic until tonight." Pacey finally reveals the anger inside him, which is unfortunately directed at Joey. The sight of Joey and Dawson dancing would be romantic if it were not for Pacey and Gretchen's eyes boring into them. Pacey's furious with Joey: "... being with you makes me feel like I'm worthless, and stupid, and never right..." He adds that he can't bear to touch her and Joey's devastated and humiliated in a room full of people. Dawson – without even thinking about Gretchen – follows her outside. When he returns, Gretchen realizes: "I need to go on with my life. Go back to college. Figure out who I am, and what I want." Dawson is heartbroken.

Pacey feels as if he no longer has anything to give Joey. "You've spent your whole life trying to escape Capeside, Joey... but I *am* Capeside....You deserve better than this place, you deserve better than me."

Episode Music

Fastball – 'You're An Ocean'
Josh Joplin Group – 'I've Changed'
Eva Trout – 'Ruby's Gone'
Dig Deeper – 'Talk Show'
Ego – 'Sun Drop'
Tish Hinojosa – 'Roses Around My Feet'
k.d. lang – 'When We Collide'
Vagabond Lovers – 'Wonderful Thing'
Mary Beth – 'Aftershocks'
Sid Six – '20one'
Dido – 'Take My Hand'
Everett Bradley – 'Whadify'

Separation Anxiety .... Episode #421
Written by Rina Mimoun
Directed by Krishna Rao

Who is leaving whom, exactly?

Drue's taking bets on which couple, Pacey and Joey or Dawson and Gretchen, will get back together. Neither couple has spoken, with Gretchen and Pacey avoiding all eyes in their beach house. Gale informs Dawson that Gretchen is leaving town: "if you want to keep Gretchen in your life, you need to talk to her," she advises. When he confronts Gretchen, Dawson's mad but relents when she admits to how difficult she would have found it to say goodbye.

Joey runs into the Worthington rep Mr Kubelik and has then to find the guts to approach Pacey and tell him that he is invited, along with some local freshmen, to a meet and greet. She's stunned at Pacey's interruption: "I miss you, Joe." Pacey tells Gretchen that if he is given an offer for Worthington, he will take it as a sign that he and Joey should be together. Joey's not as uncomfortable as she was at the first Worthington meeting. Pacey's floored when he learns the great offer he envisioned turns out to be a summer job as a deck-hand on the Dean of Admission's boat. Joey's equally upset and, although Pacey wants her to remain at the party, she leaves with him. In the morning, he expresses his regret at turning into "the stereotypical guy who can't handle the fact that his girlfriend has a better job than him."

Dawson's aiming to complete his Brooks film soon to enable him to join USC's summer programme. Realizing what an inspiration Brooks was, he tells Gretchen he wants to go with her. "I've got this feeling in my gut telling me that this is our moment, Gretchen. We can't just let it slip by." She's stunned

Jen to Grams:
"When it comes to romance, you've had more action this year than I've had. You're the youngest grandmother I know."

but unable to find adequate reasons why he shouldn't go. Writing a goodbye letter, Dawson's unable to conjure up an explanation for his disappearance. Gretchen pops round to see how Dawson's preparations are going but his wistful expression tells her much. Next morning, he realizes she has gone without him, leaving a note in his yearbook saying he needs to enjoy the rest of his time in Capeside.

Jen's shocked to learn that not only has Grams put the house on the market to fund Jen's education, but she also wants to move to a retirement home. Jen is adamant she wants to check out the retirement home as well. After the visit, she insists Grams is not moving there, not selling the house and instead, she will postpone Boston. Jack is not as furious as Jen thought he would be, but neither is he speechless: "It's as if you're happy to have found something that gets you off the hook so you don't have to go away to college." Jen spends the night thinking and comes up with the compromise of asking Grams to move to Boston with her.

Dawson and Joey come to an understanding that their friendship remains. They can be honest about their moods with each other, without having to fake it.

Episode Music

Mud'l Head – 'Dead Yet'
Jessica Andrews – 'Show Me Heaven'
Edwin McCain – 'Write Me A Song'
Amy Cook – 'Windows'
Shawn Colvin – 'One Small Year'
Mark Kozolek – 'Around And Around'
Colin Hay – 'Waiting For My Real Life To Begin'

The Graduate .... Episode #422
Written by Alan Cross
Directed by Harry Winer

Pacey's drowning and unwilling for anyone to save him. He has to save himself.

The Capeside High graduation rehearsal is in full swing when Mitch has the unpleasant job of telling Pacey his grades are still borderline – his final exam will be the decider and he needs to go and study for it. It's a humiliating walk past his buddies.

With Joey winning the Capeside Pinnacle Award, she has to make a speech. Cue mental block. Dawson thinks it's Pacey-inspired and she needs to try harder to get him to accept her help. Next morning, just before his exam, Pacey blows up, saying teachers don't care about the underachievers, just the honor students: "... maybe I am an idiot. Because I can't for the life of me figure out why I'm trying so goddamn hard." And with that, he storms out of the test. When Joey asks him to let her help him, he's reluctant. "As much as I'd like the concept of being 'just friends', in reality it's this bizarre form of torture." Imagine Pacey's surprise when Mr Kasdan turns up at the beach house, with the test and a pencil, inviting Pacey to remind him why he went into teaching; to help kids just like him.

Jen to Drue:
"You get one night. On the floor. And don't even think about sleeping naked."
Drue:
"Fair enough, though keep in mind I impose no such restriction on you."

Back home, Joey still has no luck with her speech. Bessie gives her a letter their mom wrote before she passed away – and it is Dawson she asks to read it as she's too frozen. It's a heart-warming ode to the woman Joey has become with a word of wisdom to "keep close those who shared your childhood".

There was Tobey worried Jack couldn't even say the word "boyfriend", when he up and uses the word when introducing him to Andie. Everyone's surprised at her return, especially Pacey who smiles for the first time in a long time. He reveals he's contemplating the sailing job offer and also... that he passed his final. When, finally, he speaks to Joey, he asks if she would ever consider sailing with him and she replies: "You wouldn't have to ask." Next day, while everyone prepares for graduation, Pacey is packing, preparing to leave town, to leave Capeside for the summer.

Following a flaming row with his mother, Drue requests sleepover permission at Jen's house. She acquiesces with "hands to yourself" conditions. The next day, when Jen sees Drue sharing tea with Grams, she's unnecessarily concerned. "I'm not a naïve old softie dear," says Grams privately, "I recognize Drue for the duplicitous, smooth-talking, butt-kisser he is." Grams forgot "troublesome" as he attempts to "sprinkler" the graduation crowd, and gets both himself and Jen busted by Peskin. Their punishment is particularly inventive; Peskin forces them to listen to his chillingly bad cello recital.

Graduation is a time for friends and family alike to be proud. The gang have worked hard and deserve all they receive. But while Joey is making her speech, Pacey is departing. She comments on how everyone who attended Capeside High will take a little of the town with them, wherever they are heading.

Episode Music

Barenaked Ladies – 'Pinch Me'
Robbie Williams – 'If It's Hurting You'
Amy Dalley – 'Dream Too Small'
Dragmatic – 'If'
Jann Arden – 'Good Mother'
Eva Cassidy – 'Fields of Gold'

Coda .... Episode #423
Written by Gina Fattore & Tom Kapinos
Directed by Greg Prange

The return of the Movie Night as we know it.

With school pressure off, what remains of the gang simply hangs out, reminiscing. Joey says to Gale: "Sometimes you just get so wrapped up in things, you can't see the forest for the melodrama."

Sea Creature From The Deep flickers, while Dawson and Joey discuss the quick passage of time. (See Pilot Episode #100 to watch the cast making this Dawson classic). Dawson's hankering after a Mac has no bearing on his dad, who buys him a PC. As Dawson heads out to the pictures, Mitch opines: "You'd rather go to the movies than spend what little time you have left with myself, your mother, and your baby sister?" Gale warns Mitch later to confront his fears rather than make a row, especially with Dawson about to leave.

Jack forces Dawson to think about spending the summer in Capeside, with Joey. "I fell in love with someone else this year. Do you have any idea how

Joey to Dawson:

"The past couple of years... it's been this soap opera. I wouldn't change any of it – I wouldn't – but I'm glad it's over. I like how things feel now."

significant that is for me? But why can't I stop thinking about her?" Meanwhile, Jen is making Joey think about making Dawson stay in town for the summer. Dawson and Joey's goodbyes are plain, simple. It's earthy Bessie who makes Joey think if she would be satisfied with the departure if his plane "... went down in a fiery crash", and she wouldn't.

Saying goodbye to Jack and Jen, Dawson adds to his electronic collection as they give him a cell phone: "It was either that or a BMW," Jack quips before Dawson heads home. There, Mitch has bought him a Mac, as he wanted, and more importantly, owns up to how he'll miss his first-born. On board a boat, somewhere tropical, Pacey calls his best friend. "I called because I wanted you to know that despite everything that's happened and all the miles between us right now, I still think about the way it was in the beginning."

Grams is leaving the home she once shared with her husband, and though Jack and Jen expect her to be a little downhearted about it, she isn't. "... it's strangely exhilarating..."

Episode Music

Eels – 'Packing Blankets'
Jill Sobule – 'Rock Me To Sleep'
Natalie Merchant – 'How You've Grown'
Mary Beth – 'Daydream Believer'

Neither Dawson nor Joey felt the goodbye was adequate and she turns up in her rowboat, just like yesteryear, except there's no longer any ladder into his room. She helps him to pack, then, after they have refreshed each other's memories about various life-moments, Joey reveals the most incredible moment she's experienced so far in her life: "I was standing over there, by the window. And you kissed me. And it changed everything." They finally work out a way to say goodbye.

Who's Kissed Whom?

Who would ever have thought that Capeside High would have to start auctioning kisses to get a little lip-action going in the small town? We take an amusing look at the pecks and full on smooches of our favourites, including antics which we were previously not privy to.

Dawson	Jen – following his redundant attempt to film their first kiss, he and Jen share a scorcher, Episode #102, *Kiss*
	Joey – their second kiss was while Joey was inebriated in Episode #107, *Boyfriend*
	Nina – film-buff girl in *Film Threat* T-shirt from Episode #108, *Road Trip*
	Eve – the first kiss is in a janitor's closet, but they go on to more action in front of the capacity-filled auditorium in Episode# 302, *Homecoming*
	Kate – Jack's ex-girlfriend who promptly vomits after the event! Episode #314, *Valentine's Day Massacre*
	Joey – Dawson had planned a perfect evening for Episode #322, *The Anti-Prom*, and shows her with a peck how he wanted it to end
	Gretchen – the beginning was down to a bunch of mistletoe in Episode #409, *Kiss Kiss Bang Bang*
	Joey – after all the back and forth, the pair finally work out a simple and sweet way to bid adieu. Episode #423, *Coda*
Joey	Anderson – rich young tourist Joey romances in appropriately named Episode #102, *Kiss*

Dawson – the first time, most famously, due to Abby Morgan's Truth or Dare game during Episode #106, *Detention*

Pacey – after seeing her undressing after their snail trail in Episode #110, *Double Date*, Pacey pecked her but Joey was uninterested

Jack – The first time – notoriously – while she was still Dawson's girlfriend, Episode #205, *Full Moon Rising*

A.J. – considering how they started off thinking the other was the opposite sex, the kiss was interesting. Episode #313, *Northern Lights*

Pacey – judging by the number of punches she gave him in return, she was not happy, Episode #317, *Cinderella Story*

Pacey – altogether different as she returned the secret kiss, Episode #319, *Stolen Kisses*

Dawson – an unrequited kiss, Episode #322, *The Anti-Prom*

Drue – he snatches a kiss as payment for saving Joey from a fall, Episode #411, *The Tao of Dawson*

Dawson – Episode #423, *Coda*

Pacey	Joey – Episode #110, *Double Date*
	Jen – Episode #106, *Detention*, much to Dawson's anger

Pacey	Ms Tamara Jacobs – this sassy teacher taught more than the differences between similes and metaphors in English Lit. and much more than how to kiss
	Andie – his first serious relationship, Episode #206, *The Dance*
	Andie – but this was the kiss of a couple on the verge of splitting up, Episode #302, *Homecoming*
	Andie – they share a night they both later regret, Episode #306, *Secrets and Lies*
	Joey – how did Pacey perceive it? Even unreciprocated it was earth-moving, Episode #317, *Cinderella Story*
	Joey – the reciprocated kiss from Episode #319, *Stolen Kisses*
Jen	The un-named older boy Jen lost her virginity to in her New York days
	Billy – ex-boyfriend, he and Jen were caught doing a lot more than kissing by her parents, hence her banishment to Capeside. Episode #104, *Hurricane*
	Dawson – Episode #102, *Kiss*
	Pacey – Another Abby escapade from Episode #106, *Detention*
	Clifford Elliot – Jen dated him three times in Season 1, Episode #101, *Dance*, then Episode #109, *The Scare*, and lastly in Episode #110, *Double Date*.; funnily enough, Dawson was present on all three occasions

Jen	Vincent – the handsome yet brutish fisherman who proved to be dangerous in Episode #205, *Full Moon Rising*
	Chris Wolfe – a bit more than a kiss if you remember Episode #207, *The All-Nighter*
	Ty – the Bible-basher proves to be the most smitten with Jen and she dates him until realizing he's a neanderthal. Episode #216, *Be Careful What You Wish For*
	Henry – even though he paid $500 for it, it still counts, Episode #304, *Home Movies*
	Henry – completely different as she initiated and he reciprocated Episode #314, *Valentine's Day Massacre*
	Jack – despite being drunk as skunks and the post-kiss regret, it still counts! Episode #414, *A Winter's Tale*
Jack	The un-named girl Jack lost his virginity to, Episode #210, *High Risk Behavior*
	Joey – Episode #205, *Full Moon Rising*
	Kate – her night in Capeside reveals much, including the revelation that she and Jack were intimate, Episode #314, *Valentine's Day Massacre*
	Ethan – following his inability to do the deed after the 'Anti-Prom' (Episode #322) he finally does it with embarrassing consequences in Episode #323, *True Love*
	Jen – says Jack tearfully afterwards: "… I'm scared I'm never gonna meet a guy that I love as much as I love you," Episode #414, *A Winter's Tale*
	Tobey – the guy Jack insists he dislikes at first, turns out to be the one for him, Episode #420, *Promicide*
Andie	Pacey – romantically and charmingly, her first, Episode #206, *The Dance*
	Pacey – it is supposed to be the kiss of a couple who have been apart, but it's distinctly unsatisfying, Episode #302, *Homecoming*
	Marc – in the same episode, we discover Andie not only kissed but slept with Marc while in the clinic
	Rob Logan – but we're not too sure that Andie is entirely truthful about what went on, even though she spends the night with Pacey afterwards, Episode #306, *Secrets and Lies*
	Jean-Jean or J.J. – American boy studying in France who shares a cool smoocher, Episode #401, *Coming Home*

Fishing for Clues: Character Profiles

Dawson Leery, Joey Potter, Pacey Witter, Jen Lindley, Jack and Andie McPhee have really come into their own over Seasons III and IV. Each has been personality tested by personal trials, the likes of which Capeside has not seen before. They have discovered and conquered fears, indulged and regretted, loved and lost, and returned to the fulfilling friendships that made them so loveable in the first place. Here, we take a look at some of the principal characters' ordeals, and assess how well they fared.

DAWSON LEERY

Played by James Van Der Beek

Has Dawson Leery changed since we were first introduced to this sensitive, self-aware and idealistic 15-year-old boy? Has he by heck. There is no way he is as idealistic as when we first met the boy who would argue that Spielberg was practically a documentary maker, capturing human emotions at their best. His life revolved in ever-decreasing circles – and though those circles were all-engaging – he seemed unaware of life beyond them. There was one circle in which his parents, on the verge of a divorce, revolved like a Disco 45. There was the circle inhabited by Dawson's infatuation, and resultant disappointment, with Jen Lindley, the sophisticate from New York. Let's not forget Pacey Witter, troubled wit, leaping from one Creek quagmire to another. And most important, there was Joey Potter. Between them, they defined and destroyed the term platonic.

Imagine the events on the Creek controlled by Greek and Roman gods of old. Our hero Dawson faces challenges thrown into his path by various gods wishing to live vicariously through this blonde-haired stripling. A "Love Goddess" has, in the form of Eve, come to tempt him and dissuade him from the

melancholy of losing Joey. The gods of "Troubles at Home" have upset this innocent with a home life not to be envied. The god of "Friendship" has torn him asunder from his former best pal Pacey. A particularly insidious blow was perhaps that struck by the goddess of "Drive and Determination". Without his Spielberg hero-worship, Dawson was adrift on the Creek, swirling aimlessly. And most cruel of all, the god of "Things That Are Not Supposed to Happen", made his best friends Joey and Pacey fall for each other. And, as if that wasn't enough, the gods eradicated Movie Night!

Being that he is a boy with his heart on his sleeve, Dawson's trials were particularly painful for him. But they were necessary for him to mature, to become a young man as opposed to the boy we first met in Season I. How did he fare?

Since we first met Eve, she was every high-school boy's dream – blonde, lissom and long-legged. Dawson actually thought he was dreaming when he first espied her. Here he is, trying to get over losing the love of his life, and there she is, offering him an opportunity to unburden himself. She is great; relaxed, non-judgmental, and the type of gal who endeavors to show Dawson there's truth to the cliché, action speaks louder than words. When they're cruising on his father's boat, his attempts to find this out founder on the rocks. But Dawson learned a little something that day. Teenagers are allowed to have fun and, at times, they may even prove a little reckless. But responsibility weighed heavy on Dawson and he began to worry about paying for the damage to Mitch's boat. Cue Eve and Pacey in their best help-a-buddy-out mode. Trust Eve to be just on the right side of sleaze. She worked in a strip club but did not disrobe for the post, in fact she actually donned a wig. With her quick thinking she saved Dawson's hide and he's more than appreciative.

Eve is everything Dawson is not, at ease with her sex drive, living for the moment, generally cool, calm and collected. She recognizes her role as a temptress and when she obtains an advance copy of the practice SAT test, she even hands Dawson a gleaming red apple in reverence of her namesake. She pushes Dawson to his limit and provides him with exactly what he needed at the time – an attractive distraction from the ever-decreasing circles of his existence. Eve gets Dawson's blood rushing. Joey recognizes Eve is everything she is not, but Dawson is giddily whirling in the way teens are sometimes supposed to. Eve teases Dawson about his status as American virgin and blatantly expresses her desire to help him shed that burden. Somewhat thankfully, Eve and Dawson never consummate their "relationship" as it was never meant to be. Even though she never picked that cherry, Eve had an indelible effect on Dawson and we can ascribe some of his later capricious behaviour to her influence.

Though Mitch and Gale were never in danger of losing their son to the dark side, were they not so engaged with their own traumas they might have noticed his flirtations with Eve were bordering on the reckless. But Mitch and Gale were so busy clarifying the parameters of their relationship that it was only when Dawson protested at his confusion about his home life, that they realized they were seriously affecting their only child with their on-again, off-again affiliation. If they weren't sharing a Potter Bed-and-Breakfast room, they were opening a business. Dawson receives excellent counsel from Nikki Green, another child of the era of divorce, and begins to accept that his family will not be a single unit again. But – unpredictable as ever – he catches his parents in a post-coital flush of tousled hair and they have to admit they are on-again. On in such a big way in fact that they remarry. There was Dawson worried about the "primary example of love" not lasting, and they get back together, just like a Motown song.

Even if Dawson was not very good at trigonometry, he should have known, being a film fan, that the triangle created by him, Joey, and Pacey was always doomed to heartbreak. After he and Joey's relationship floundered, Dawson innocently sought Pacey's friendship for Joey. Together, Dawson and Pacey paved a road of good intentions for Joey to walk gracefully along. With his vision blurred by other events in his life, Dawson can be forgiven for missing the closeness that grew between his friends. Pacey was torn, Joey was shredded – they had to justify feelings that, in any other circumstance, would have been fine – two teens in love. Without his even knowing, Dawson became an albatross around the couple's neck. The discovery though, cued heartbreak for three. He was devastated. Though he is a sensitive lad, there have only been a few times since we've known him that he has truly sunken into melancholy (his break-up with Jen, his parent's divorce). After all, he has always had his eternal idealism to parachute him to emotional safety. Cruelly ironic though, he is in the process of losing this childish trait when this blow knocks him sideways. The sense of betrayal lingered in the air like ozone after a thunder storm.

The question "how?" may as well have been tattooed on poor Dawson's forehead. For a while, he was bitter, twisted, jealous. He issued ultimatums and was decidedly ugly when he spat: "… if you choose Pacey, I won't be there to pick up the pieces when it falls apart," to a heartbroken Joey. But eventually, he realized, with Gretchen's help, that he cannot control everything in his life, the world does not revolve around him. Dawson eventually rebuilds his relationship with Joey, though it's not the same. With Pacey, it's more fraught. Though Dawson saves his buddy's life, they are slower to rekindle a friendship many would envy. But this trial taught Dawson his most powerful lesson, in learning to accept changes, however difficult.

A particular trial for Dawson, his loss of ambition, came at a time when he should have been gleefully perusing college prospectuses, taking his pick of film schools across the country. Instead Dawson discovered there were life trials Spielberg seems not to have addressed in his movies. Dawson was stuck without his posters, without the drive we had come to love. And along came Arthur Brooks, the meanest, most sarcastic wrinkled collection of put-downs ever to wake a teen up to the fact that he needs to get over himself. Never in the history of the Creek has someone stopped Dawson mid-self-analytical flow so abruptly: "Teenage angst gives me heartburn." Despite his temper, his sometimes poisonous view of the world, Brooks gave Dawson much to think about in a short space of time, including the temporarily forgotten reasons to pick up a film camera.

So, the gods threw their worst at a boy named Dawson and he emerged victorious – a man. He is surer of himself, more accepting of things he has little influence upon. At the end of his journey, he returns home to find a beautiful baby sister, Lillian, and a soulmate, Joey, who he had never really lost at all. The Creek's ripples no longer represent his life and he is on his way to forge a history and a story of his own making.

JOEY POTTER
Played by Katie Holmes

Movement has always defined Josephine Potter. She rowed across the Creek to find her best pal Dawson for Movie Night. She shimmied across the bed when platonic became a term ever more difficult to define. As a waitress at the family restaurant that burnt down, The Ice House, she would waltz between the tables, laden with a tray. More recently, she would skitter after her sister Bessie's baby, Alexander, as he sought something babies should not. And she would shudder around in the family truck, determined as anything to get the hang of the stick shift.

Joey's only moments of stillness were dedicated to study. Ironically, the aim of her studies was to open a chance of permanent escape from Capeside. She made Escape From Capeside sound like a 50s B-movie, so grim were her melancholic predictions: "I am doomed to roam the streets of Capeside for all eternity." Perhaps one of the reasons for Joey's insistence about her need to escape the town centers on how indecisive she seems to be when she is in town. When she steps outside its boundaries, we recognize the traits of an intelligent, articulate young woman. Joey wounded her sister with her insistence that she did not want to be like her, stuck in the town of their birth. But later she retracted her harsh words by clarifying that she wanted different opportunities.

At the start of Season III, Joey was still in a tender state, following her break-up with Dawson. Her soulmate had caused her father – someone she loved dearly, drug dealer though he was – to be sent to prison, and they both needed time apart to deal with the ramifications of such a hideous occurrence. Having not seen him all summer, Joey made the mistake of throwing herself at Dawson, only to be humiliated by his refusal. He was forced to remind her that it was "not the same any more." And there the conflict arose that we see etched across her brow so often. She was forever drawn to Dawson, but until they had both reached a point of true reconciliation, any relationship, be it friendship or more, was bound to be difficult. Dawson though, ever wise, requested Pacey to keep an eye on Joey, ensuring she had a reliable friend when she needed one in his absence. And though Joey was furious when she found out about this arrangement a little later, she knew inside that this was why Dawson was someone who only ever had her best interests at heart for, in the midst of his own turmoil, he always thought of her.

Dawson and Joey's relationship has always been fraught with problems. From the first episode where she warned Dawson that the flood of hormones teens experience would make their platonic relationship a rougher terrain, to the time when they managed to get it together but realized that, while emotions had run high, nothing groundbreaking had really happened. But, as even Joey admits, Dawson's room is like a safe house for her, somewhere she can bounce ideas around without feeling imbecilic, a place of true friendship she is drawn to in times of need. Imagine, then, how difficult it was for her to have this safety net removed. She had concerns enough to keep her busy but the growing pains she was so used to discussing with Dawson were gone, and the vacuum was like that of space.

Step in Pacey. While Dawson and Joey's relationship was always based on a not-so-subtle subtext, Pacey and Joey's relationship was born of banter snappier than a snapping turtle. More than anyone, it was gritty Pacey who would tell Joey to simply get over herself. With a wry grin, he would turn her frown to a smirk with a self-deprecating remark and, despite bumping into Dawson on occasion, she actually began to get on with the business of enjoying life and relaxing. Though Joey herself had nightmares about never getting away from the small town, Pacey shared his dreams of her glittering future with her.

But it was not only one way. Make no mistake, Joey as a friend is a prize catch. Yes, you have to put up with the constant hair-flicking and eye-rolling, but there are worse personal habits. She is as smart as a whip and aided Pacey in his failing classes. In Boston, though humiliated by A.J. for liking *Little Women* by Louisa May Alcott, Joey later goes on to develop a relationship with him. He is intelligent, witty and artistic – the mirror-image of Dawson, in fact. Unfortunately, the mirror-image is perfect even to the detail of having a female soulmate. Joey is heartbroken and it is a concerned Pacey who picks her up from the train station.

Pacey worked so clever a spell of rejuvenating Joey's spirit that she failed to notice that she and Pacey had begun to create a sub-text of their own. Pacey confided in his brother about his feelings for Joey, but she remained unaware. Pacey even spilled the beans to his mentee, Buzz, but Joey remained ignorant. The first she knew of anything was when he planted his lips on hers, on the drive back from Boston. The very first time Joey was kissed by Pacey, way back in Episode #110, *Double Date*, she calmly assured him that though they were friends, they were nothing more. This time, Joey whacks him and protests and protests and protests – until Jen informs her she is protesting too much. This gives Joey pause for thought. The resultant decision – to pretend the kiss was merely an "impulse" – is far from believable. When she and Pacey accept their feelings and contemplate ways of telling Dawson, the strain begins to show in Joey's face. She never imagined she would ever play the role of a *femme fatale* in the Creek's own version of a film noir.

Dawson's thunderstruck face when he works out the truth is a bitter blow to Joey. She was beginning to enjoy his friendship when, yet again, they were cleaved apart by circumstances beyond her control. In time though, Dawson forgave her, but not Pacey. Joey, therefore, was stuck in limbo between the combative pair. It was painful but eased by the attentions of Pacey. And boy, was he attentive. Though fiercely independent, when the need arose he was there for Joey. When the thuggish Matt Caufield defaces her mural, it was Pacey who put his "future on the line" in order to discover the truth. Even though he

does not really understand her belief that "art has power" he rents her a wall and invites her to rise to the challenge. She is highly appreciative.

When Joey finally, finally accepts that she has truly fallen in love with someone other than Dawson, she begins to realize that, though her life is complicated, she deserves some happiness. She takes the leap and loses her virginity to Pacey. And though she mistakenly lies to protect Dawson from the painful truth, not that it's any of his damned business, she and Pacey fleetingly, briefly, glimpse true happiness. The relationship is cathartic for both. She assures Pacey that her love is true and reminds him that no one else would have whisked her away for the summer, no-one else would have threatened their own future to capture Caufield, no-one else would have challenged her with a brick wall, and no-one teaches stick shift like Pacey, or cracks a joke like him.

But Joey is constantly on the move remember? Pacey, struggling with school, realizes – perhaps before Joey – that their time is soon to end. She is able to accept Dawson's money to enable her to go to Worthington, the college she has dreamed of attending. She is also able to accept Pacey's depar- ture gracefully, knowing that what they shared was not a substitute but something she needed to enable her to progress. With Dawson, she reaches a new understanding that echoes the touching letter her mother had written for her before she passed away. Regardless of where their futures may carry them, they will always cherish the friends they had in Capeside, the town Joey may be desperate to leave, but one that she will hopefully return to with happy memories.

PACEY WITTER
Played by Joshua Jackson

Pacey has always sought to live up to his surname, even in times of stress. He is the one who makes with the mirth while Dawson loses himself in introspection, the one who lifts Jen from her mire, the savior of Andie who too often feels she has to be perfect, the one who just lets Joey be Joey in the face of conflicting demands placed upon her.

Surely then, it was a truly defining moment when Pacey lamented: "No-one is there for Pacey," a comment made more poignant as it was his birthday. It was the lowest point for someone whom we have grown to love because of his positive outlook on life. He didn't have Dawson's idealism to fall back on, but he had an indefatigable belief that things would be all right at the end. A number of events had thrown Pacey into the kind of turmoil lesser personalities may not have survived. But with his inner strength – the kind our standardized testing education system takes little heed of – and friends who really were there for him, he pulled through admirably.

During the course of Season III, Pacey learned that his first love Andie betrayed him. He could barely fathom it. He had awaited her return from hospital with bated breath. Yes, he had also spent much of the summer in a strip club, but that's Pacey and you gotta love him for it. Cast your minds way back to Episode #206, *The Dance*, when he and Andie first got it together. He was following a high-

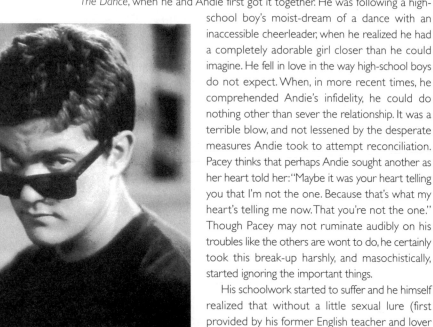

school boy's moist-dream of a dance with an inaccessible cheerleader, when he realized he had a completely adorable girl closer than he could imagine. He fell in love in the way high-school boys do not expect. When, in more recent times, he comprehended Andie's infidelity, he could do nothing other than sever the relationship. It was a terrible blow, and not lessened by the desperate measures Andie took to attempt reconciliation. Pacey thinks that perhaps Andie sought another as her heart told her: "Maybe it was your heart telling you that I'm not the one. Because that's what my heart's telling me now. That you're not the one." Though Pacey may not ruminate audibly on his troubles like the others are wont to do, he certainly took this break-up harshly, and masochistically, started ignoring the important things.

His schoolwork started to suffer and he himself realized that without a little sexual lure (first provided by his former English teacher and lover Tamara Jacobs, then McPhee) he was finding meeting his grade requirements more than a little difficult. Irony is, most people recognize that Pacey is smart as anything. What he actually finds difficult is the regimented approach to education; the sitting in rows, the having to raise your hand in order to answer a question, the meeting of deadlines. Could he survive on his wits alone while sailing the coasts? You betcha. But, there was a little sexual lure in store for Pacey, even though the provider of the lure wanted – at first – nothing to do with it.

Considering he was "taking care" of Joey for his pal Dawson, Pacey didn't have to go far for a study partner. She provided him with trigonometry coaching, he crushed her toes in dancing class. But then, with all that hand clasping and swooping and cha-cha-cha-ing, Pacey began to develop a crush on Joey. And here we are with the trigonometry again. The hypotenuse, the adjacent and the opposite creating three sides that would be torn asunder once it was discovered what was occurring at one angle of the triangle. Joey, at first, would not reciprocate. She protested and within each sentence of protest there was the name "Dawson". It was Pacey – and not out of selfishness – who asked her to stop and think about what Joey wanted for a moment. And Joey wanted and needed Pacey.

Joey to Pacey: (reading from *The Little Mermaid*) **"The little mermaid could not take her eyes from the ship, or from the beautiful prince."**

Cast your minds way back to when Pacey had actually sought Dawson's permission to pursue Joey in Episode #110, *Double Date*. Was it serious? Who knows? But Pacey was a little smitten following a chance sighting of a nude Joey as she undressed near his rear-view mirror. At the time, Dawson and Joey were beginning to realize things were getting complicated between them but imagine how Dawson would have reacted had Pacey sought his permission? Dawson was in a ditch of his own making at the time though. He was finding a relationship with the girl of his dreams impossibly difficult and would not have been impressed by Pacey approaching him, cap in hand. But then again, Joey had always caused a little friction between Pacey and Dawson. Indeed, Pacey had, on the occasion when Dawson forgot his birthday, said: "Everything is different now. You have Joey and our friendship can't compete with what you and Joey have. And I'm not the third wheel type."

This time though, it was Dawson who would become the "third wheel type." Pacey was drawn toward Joey like iron filings to a magnet. What should have been a time of love, pure and simple, instead became a moment of ambivalence. There was love unabated for Joey, but a sense of betrayal that lingered and lingered. It should have been a time for a jaded Pacey to recognize that he could love again – but it was so much more complicated. He and Dawson shared the kind of idyllic male friendship Stephen King writes about; they fished, they camped in the woods, the old lady with the dog chased them off her land. But it was more than that. Pacey and Dawson were brothers.

It was heartbreaking to see Pacey's helplessness in falling for the girl his best friend considered his soulmate. Pacey would "…daydream about a world where I had my own bathroom, my mom was on TV, and my dad was like a superhero." He never imagined though, in any nightmare, being able to prevent himself from loving his best friend's love. And of course, Dawson would, though unintentionally, periodically make Pacey feel like crawling away. On their weekend at his aunt's house, Dawson says: "Once upon a time, Pacey Witter was the town screw-up. Glib, lazy, predictable. Then you changed. I thought for a while it was your relationship with Andie. But you're not with her now and you're still… well, thank you… for taking care of Joey."

Once Dawson realized he and Pacey were pursuing the same girl – and let's face it, Dawson was pursuing Joey in a slow, methodical way even while Pacey had been asked to look after her – barriers flew up. Had Dawson resorted to fists, it would have been almost acceptable. But he sulked and he seethed and he almost smashed Pacey's *True Love* against the rocks during the Capeside Regatta. Dawson found it easier to forgive Joey than he did Pacey and the sudden absence of a best friend left another hole in Pacey's life.

Pacey lost *True Love*, and he lost his best friend Dawson. Despite loving Joey as best he could, he knew – even before she did – that he would eventually lose her. It was becoming more difficult to maintain the wit of his repute. Though there was some succor to be had in the improved relationship between himself and his brother and sister, Doug and Gretchen, he still found himself, against his will, being ushered through a door of melancholy.

And then, with a sense of timing more commonly associated with a Hollywood action movie, Pacey began to pull himself together. He realized people were there for him and he began to accept some assistance. Doug and Gretchen advised him more and teased him less. Even Pacey's dad forced his son to recognize his worth. He and Dawson began to speak as opposed to grunt at each other. Andie, growing stronger within herself, finally got over Pacey, and assured him they could be true friends.

Unfortunately, Pacey's plagued by insecurity. He says to Joey: "… being with you makes me feel like I'm worthless, and stupid, and never right…" and despite her assurances to the contrary, it is obvious their time is drawing to a close. Painful as this is, the mere existence of the relationship was confirmation that he could and would love again. They needed to go their separate ways to forge their own histories. Once they both accepted this, it made the pain a little easier to bear. They were as mutually beneficial to each other as they could have been and at least they parted on good terms.

And, independent spirit that he is, Pacey managed to prevent himself from failing high school. There are few things worse than seeing someone with potential let it slip away from them. Any teacher could tell you a tale or two about promising pupils who blunder their way to educational failure. Luckily for Pacey, Mr Kasdan was not going to let him be an addition to the drop-out list. Pacey passed high school and left town quietly. Not every hero receives a fanfare worthy of a Lucas film at the end of their adventures.

No, Pacey's adventures did not end with bags packed, ready to go to further education and beer keg parties, and random safe-sex. But he was our only gang member who literally sailed off into a sunset. He left a young man, with happy memories, a few belongings, a bright future ahead, and his interminable wit intact.

JEN LINDLEY
Played by Michelle Williams

Of all the characters in Capeside, Jen is perhaps the one most troubled by ghosts from her past. Jen may have believed she did a really good job of reinventing herself upon her arrival in Capeside, but it came to pass that, despite having lines most comedians would sell a body part for, she began to suffer. Unable to view her past without anger, Jen became frightened of – and started to sabotage – her own future.

But hey, even though Capeside is not New York, that doesn't mean it doesn't boast its own gang of ghostbusters. And, they're a damned sight better-looking and better-equipped than the originals for busting the kind of ghosts that inhabited Jen's mind and fed off unhappy thoughts and repressed memories.

First and foremost, there is Jack, Jen's best friend. He's the trusty male sidekick Jen never thought she would have, as most men, to her, were not trusty and not even that good for kicking either. Being gay, Jack had no interest in getting in her knickers, and instead would offer good advice and the chance to lay around in the park getting soaked by the sprinklers. This is the kind of thing underrated in therapy circles; it's immensely cleansing and good for the

pores, too. In Jack, Jen had a male figure of trust. As time went on, we discovered the disturbing specter of Jen's father and could more easily understand her trust issues. All the more reason for Jack to be commended, as he himself, of course, had issues with his father as well.

If you check Jen's kissing action during Seasons I and II, it's obvious she was a popular girl, but during Seasons III and IV, something happened. Jen was no longer the girl who would throw herself into relationships before checking out the guy's intentions, as well as his butt. Someone worthy did come along but jaded as Jen was, he would not have stood a chance if it had not been for the machinations of Jack. He would not set his best friend up with an unworthy type and, knowing how insanely in love Henry Parker was, he hooked the pair together. Henry was a delight to Jen. He strove to be the "most original person" in Jen's life and he was. He was so honest it petrified her. He was so forthright, he troubled her. He was so in love, he frightened her. "You're this strange and wonderful boy, a genre unto yourself. What if the gods finally figure out I don't deserve you?"

Considering how damned terrified she actually was of him, it's amazing she returned his love, wholeheartedly. When Henry disappointed her with his ill-timed impression of an amorous octopus, Jen feared he was just like all the other lads she had dated, interested in only one thing. Yes, Henry was interested in sex but he also appreciated Jen for her personality, wit, and charm, and apologized endlessly to prove this. It then transpired that Henry would be going away to football school for the entire summer and Jen, needy kind of gal that she is, pondered how he could bear to be apart for so long. But for Grams' sound advice, that would have been the end of the tale of Henry and Jen. In a grand, sweeping gesture, Jen chased Henry down highways and byways and in front of his football buddies, declared her love and assured him she could wait. It was a moment to bring a lump to the throat of even the most jaded. Ironically though, he couldn't. She had lost someone dear to her and began to sink in a mire of melancholy.

The Lindley lass began to drink, miss classes, and, while everyone ran around frantically, filling in college applications, she lounged on her bed and listened to chick rock. Drue Valentine's appearance in town did not help. Her past New York indiscretion was witty but still stuck on this childish good-time roll, desperate to relive the Agony and the Ecstasy of what he perceived to be the good ol' days. Jen's indifference to life was a cloud that traveled with her wherever she could be bothered to drag her heavy feet. The funk lasted until Grams could take it no longer.

Having being sent to Capeside for various indiscretions, Grams was just the sort of strict disciplinarian Jen needed at the time. There were curfews, religious lectures and frowns at short skirts. But as Jen grew, Grams' parenting took on a new dimension. Every now and again, she would shock Jen out of her "know it all arrogance" with a personal tale to give her grand-daughter pause for thought. Coming from a dysfunctional family, Jen was unused to such honesty and appreciated it. If it were not for Grams, Jen would not have borne her mother's visit to Capeside. Helen Lindley was barely in town for a day but Jen came to a new understanding of her mother. She had been through the same teen rebellious phase Jen was experiencing but had given birth to a daughter. Jen was at first scorched by the hypocrisy of the incident. Cast your minds way back to Episode #221, *Ch–ch–changes*, where Jen had begged to be allowed to return to New York but was refused. After reflection though, Jen saw something in her mother - a sad, lonely woman stuck in a loveless marriage - that elicited pity and forgiveness. Another ghost conquered.

Grams continued to be the dependable, trustworthy adult Jen needed. It may at first have been thought that Jen had been irrevocably damaged by the actions of her parents, sending her away from home in her moment of need, but it turned out to be Jen's saving. She was given a new opportunity in a new town and through the vigilant efforts of a parental figure without a competing personal agenda, Jen succeeded in dragging herself up by her bootstraps. When Grams assumed Jen was slipping into her old ways, having spent the night with Henry, Jen was incredibly hurt. This was a perfect example of how mistaken disapproval could damage an innocent. Grams may be mature but she's still flexible enough to admit her errors. Though they had their ups and downs, Grams proved to be the kind of immovable rock for Jen that she reads about in her Bible. Even Jen, supposedly proud agnostic, admitted to believing in a higher power when she was in fear for her life, being thrown around *True Love* in the midst of the storm. She made Grams proud by saying she had lent

her grand-daughter her faith in her time of need.

By far the biggest surprise Grams gave Jen, though, was her willingness to sell the house so that Jen could attend college. Though Jen's parents are wealthy, requesting their financial support would have been out of the question because of the depth of the parent-child rift. And with Jack moving to Boston as well, it looked as if Jen was likely to continue to be surrounded by people who loved her without question.

But if things had simply ended this way, there would have remained a tremendously powerful phantom roaming free amidst the detritus of Jen's young life. Her father, a tremendously charming despot, began to haunt Jen once she started therapy sessions. When Joey accompanied Jen to New York, even she was swayed by the mellifluous verbal abilities of the king of New York. And Joey, having once mistaken the lies of her own father for the truth, was a sharp cookie when it came to being able to suss out such a duplicitous figure.

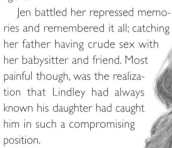

Jen battled her repressed memories and remembered it all; catching her father having crude sex with her babysitter and friend. Most painful though, was the realization that Lindley had always known his daughter had caught him in such a compromising position.

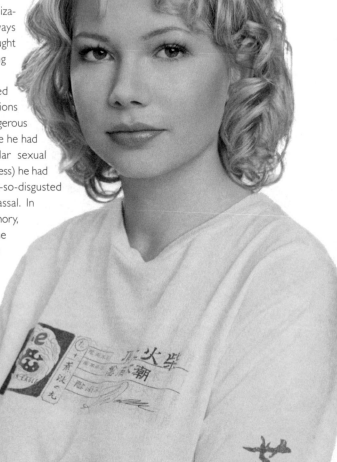

Despite this, he watched the repercussions of his actions send his daughter on a dangerous cycle of drugs and sex. Once he had discovered her in a similar sexual predicament (in his bed, no less) he had dismissed her from his oh-so-disgusted sight like an unworthy vassal. In defeating this repressed memory, Jen effectively stripped all the power from her father. She returned triumphant to Capeside and could at last look to the future with hope, all demons vanquished.

JACK McPHEE
Played by Kerr Smith

I t is commendable that Jack refuses to be defined solely in terms of his sexuality. Yes, Jack is gay – but there's more to him than that. And this is what has been so interesting about Jack's character. He did not come strutting out; he emerged as a gay young man after a series of personal trials. His relationship with Joey (Jack was the one who first split up Joey and Dawson), the ambiguous letter he penned about male attraction, and the irrational homophobic fears of his father, all tested Jack's character. He dealt with these incidents as any teen in the town of Capeside deals with them, through introspection and the assistance of good friends. As time elapsed, he has grown more assured of himself and his place in a world that is sometimes bitter, sometimes sweet. Jack McPhee is the solid, dependable guy who takes a little while to get his head around certain situations, his being gay being no exception.

So, as well as being gay, he is the best brother Andie could hope to have, offering the kind of counsel some people pay good money for. To Jen, he is the dependable bloke with the broad shoulders she can cry or laugh upon. Delightfully, he has grown into the kind of son his father knew he could be proud of. Most importantly though, Jack has certainly grown to love himself, a vital step before you can begin to love anyone else properly.

When Andie returned from her stay in the mental hospital to find she had destroyed her much-needed relationship with Pacey, she needed a brother more than ever. Her breakdown had been partially induced by the loss of her elder brother Tim, and she needed the remaining one to stabilize her. It might have seemed selfish of Jack to remain living at Grams' house, where he had moved following paternal strife, but it was necessary for his peace of mind. As it transpired, it also helped Andie to become more independent. Jack was ever-present when she needed someone to talk to regarding her problems, but she came into her own while living with her father; making mistakes and dealing with them, but ultimately finding her path.

But it is definitely a symbiotic relationship that exists between Jack and Andie. The help was mutual. She would ask Jack the difficult questions about his sexuality and urge him into those "deep breath" situations like going on his first date with a guy. This guy had seen the documentary that Dawson had made about Jack being the only gay footballer in Capeside High's Minutemen – which in itself was the leap of an increasingly confident young man. Though the date seemed a good idea at first, things progressed too fast for Jack's liking and he completely flaked, losing the confidence he had striven so hard to build. But that's the great thing with people like Andie, they not only push themselves, but those around them as well, and she continued to urge him to actively seek a relationship.

Jack is equally as brother-like to Jen. Their domestic dance at Grams' house is intriguing to watch although it pains Andie as it shows how "at home" he is away from the McPhee house. Jen and Jack's relationship originally grew from their mutual need for each other. They shared many things, from a sense of being unwanted, to a particularly jaded outlook on life. As time went on though, the Bitter Pair managed to gain a better perspective on things. Jen was introduced to Henry through Jack and Jack was introduced to football through Henry. Jen, to give credit where it's due, strove to ensure that Jack did not get depressed about the thought of never having a romantic life. Jack and Jen's relationship is almost wrecked when he discovers that Jen was partially responsible for Andie taking Ecstasy. It is through Andie's mediation though that his "surrogate sister" is returned to him.

When Jen and Jack are drunk, lonely, and more than a little randy during the senior ski trip, their closeness gets dangerous as they almost consummate what would have been a relationship doomed to failure. It is Jen who resists: "You're drunk and you're lonely and you're gay." They are destined to be friends, not lovers, as well Jack knows. Next morning, a sober Jen quips: "What if I had gotten pregnant and we had to drop out of school in our senior year to raise our illegitimate love child?" An unsettling thought.

Though he had no problems kissing Jen (drunk, mind you) ironically it's when he's sober that Jack has problems with the people he likes romantically, namely Ethan. He meets him on a train and is instantly attracted to the wiser prep school student. But the relationship was fraught with problems. Namely, Jack's shyness. It could be said that Ethan educated him in a way, insisting that Jack be a little more proactive, instead of reactive. When Jack invites Ethan to stay with him, he is surprised at how warmly Ethan behaves towards his dad, who is taking every opportunity to spy on the pair, who are at this stage, just friends. While Jack grinds his teeth, Ethan is vivacious and witty, discussing cars and anything else to win the older McPhee round. Though Jack's seething, Ethan has experience in this area and helps to dismiss the conversational cobwebs between father and son. A work buddy of Mr McPhee's has a dropout kid and listening to his tales of woe, McPhee realizes: "Jack is a good kid. I have got a good kid, and I don't even know him. But I want to know him ..." The reconciliation is the pivotal moment in the relationship – for both father and son.

Ethan continues to endeavor to instil confidence in Jack, but the scheme almost backfires at Jack's senior year celebrations. The suited and booted pair sit lifelessly while others enjoy the Anti-Prom. When Ethan seeks the cessation of the so-called festivities, things erupt. He challenges Jack openly to express himself: "Okay, so here we are. A lone train station. No one around. No lights. No camera. No network television to cut to commercial. It's you and me. So kiss me, Jack. I dare you." Truth or dare has never been Jack's forte and he backs down; after all the angst, he still can't bring himself to kiss the guy he has had a crush on for months. It's only later, when Jack sees Jen open her heart publicly to Henry, that

he is able to do the same for Ethan, kissing him in a moment that was as important for a teenage soap as it was for Jack. Unfortunately, it's a kiss too late as Ethan has sought the affections of his ex-boyfriend. It was a humiliating blow but one perhaps that Jack needed in order to enable him to continue his growth.

Jack was still fairly insecure when he met Tobey, effervescent leader of the Gay-Straight Teen coalition, but not nearly as insecure as at the outset of Season III. Tobey is so "out" it scares Jack. McPhee was still reeling from being sacked from the soccer coaching job and here's this bright, snappish spark who can see through the discriminatory act in the blink of an eye. Jack battles against the attraction and he and Tobey do not seem to see eye to eye. But when Tobey is beaten up and Jack insists he reports the incident to the police, Jack realizes that they are not as different as he once presumed. Simply being around each other, their mutual attraction continues to develop and with the help of Jen, Jack is able to admit that he is happy with Tobey and more importantly, worthy of a relationship of his own. At the close of Season IV we see Jack, ready to leave for Boston, content with his home life, looking toward the future with his best friend, surrogate grandmother and boyfriend. He may not play football anymore – especially not with a cast that switched arms, as indeed his did – but he's still capable of surprising his fans every now and again.

ANDIE MCPHEE
Played by Meredith Monroe

A ndie McPhee, the tireless, highly strung girl with the quick line in advice so good it was practically professional, finally proved she is actually fallible. Andie is a mix between Lisa Simpson, a Vulcan, and an artificial intelligence experiment, so organized and straight-road walking is she. Perfect hair, perfect grades, perfect teeth, perfect skin, perfect teen. Indeed, the kind of perfect teen that the Stepford Wives would love. They would have had few problems with the Andie McPhee of old except the kind that centered on periodic repair.

But no, Andie is entirely human. The way she drives herself, the way her AI personality type accepts nothing from herself but perfection, is both her greatest strength and her greatest weakness. In one of Dawson's Creek's most heart-breaking moments, the unrelenting way she drove herself led to the resurfacing of her mental illness. She had to leave Capeside and Pacey, the boy she had grown to love despite her problems, and retire for a while to a hospital to recuperate. Andie cried, Pacey cried, even the hard-hearted among us got a lump in our throats.

Her return then, should have been triumphant. But like Pacey, from the moment we saw her chatting in her usual animated style to the creepy dude Marc, we knew something was wrong. We were glad, as was Pacey, to have her back in town but once her tale of infidelity spilled out, it was understandable that they could no longer be together. Pacey was devastated. Had Andie forgotten just how much he had given of himself, how much of an inspiration Andie was to him? Perhaps she had, temporarily, but it was certainly a moment of amnesia that Andie regretted.

Perhaps, in an effort to prove to herself as much as to others that she was over Pacey, she started an ill-conceived relationship with Rob Logan. Joey, having worked with the lecherous creep for some time at Logan's Marina, had misgivings the size of a small town, but of course, we know what Andie is like when she has her sights set on something. Rob, she thought, would treat her as she deserved to be treated. The wealthy kid could wine and dine her. Unquestionably, he would know how a gentleman should behave towards a young lady. Andie has always been a classy lass and perhaps felt it was time to be treated as such.

Ironically, she can say none of this when Joey presses her for a reason as to why she is dating the creep. When Andie, surely one of the most articulate high-schoolers in the country, merely says: "He's nice," Joey spits: "So is Mr Charley the school janitor. You don't date him." But date Rob Andie did. It ended with Joey being sacked from her much-needed job. More importantly though, Andie then phoned Joey in tears and later spilled a tale to her and Pacey about Rob's un-gentlemanly amorous aggression. Pacey flies to her rescue, socks Rob, and it seems they are reunited.

But it's not to be. Pacey, independently of Joey's suspicions surrounding the whole incident, knows that it will not work – and yet again, Andie is devastated. Some time later, speaking to herself, Andie articulates just what the loss of Pacey means to her: "When I met him, it was like... a shade going up in a dark room, the light suddenly pouring in. He understood things about me, things no one else ever did, ever could. And then... just as suddenly, the room went dark again." This helps to put much of Andie's *modus operandi* into perspective. She transforms once again into the busy-bee character of old, high-kicking Tae-Bo style and power-walking Oprah-style through Capeside High's corridors.

Why Andie took the advance copy of the practice SAT test few people would understand. Out of the gang, she was the most prepared, as always. The others were plagued with various insecurities: Joey with sleepless nights; Dawson with Eve watching television while he tried to study; Pacey seeming not to care, considering his muse was gone. Andie, though, was up at the crack of dawn, cramming for a test she would have aced with or without the stolen test. To her mind though, taking the test was merely insurance.

Ironically, Andie is elected to the Disciplinary Committee, the kind of job she was made for. She enforces the rules, made in 1957 no less, so strictly that Principal Green is inundated. But this illustrates just how Andie operates. She has no more hours in her days than normal people and yet manages to accomplish so much. Partly, it is to keep herself too busy to sit and mope about Pacey, but also it is because it is part of her make-up to keep busy.

Andie impresses everyone, including lead actor Pacey, with her handling of the school play, *Barefoot In The Park*. It speaks volumes to many characters, but for Pacey and Andie it begins to show that they are moving towards closure. Unknown to Andie, though, this is the time when Pacey's feelings towards Joey have grown far beyond friendship. Though it seems Andie could do no wrong at this stage, the burden of cheating on the practice SAT has never left her, and finally become so weighty, she unloads herself to an understanding Green. He is disappointed, follows the rules and informs parties who need to know, but reassures her about her future. We can begin to see Andie struggling under the pressures of the pace she has set herself.

An unseen event on the horizon for Andie was Joey and Pacey's relationship. She seems to handle foreseen events fine, but these last-minute shocks faze her badly. She is hurt, betrayed, and even though she herself is on a date with Will, Pacey's friend, Andie spits: "Joey's never gonna love you the way she loves Dawson." Not exactly blessing the relationship. After the Anti-Prom, though, it is Andie who recognizes that Pacey truly loves Joey and she urges him to unburden himself. It's a surprise, as the most highly-strung character has accepted the relationship quicker than anyone else; the surprises with Andie never cease.

The biggest surprise of all though had to be Andie taking Ecstasy. And perhaps surprise was part of Andie's skewered reasoning. She sought to surprise others and herself, alleviate the stress of being a perfect teen, if even only momentarily. The Chemical Brothers' tunes pound heavily at the rave – and heavily fell Andie, in a fit induced by the mixture of Ecstasy and her anti-depressant medication. Her brother Jack felt most keenly his sister's plight. His fury at Jen took on gargantuan proportions and Jen, penitent though she was, could do nothing. Though Andie was all right and her father was surprisingly non-judgmental, the way her actions had affected everyone played heavily on her mind. She and Pacey redeveloped their friendship as he brought her, not flowers, but something much more pleasurable to Andie, homework.

Once she had accepted the proposal to leave town for a while (her grades being so good she could take a semester off), Andie took on board one last task before she went. Andie has always loved those Kodak moments. Whenever the group is together, she is the first one to memorize the events, as with Thanksgiving dinner at Grams' house: "I love a Charlie Brown Thanksgiving… that's the one where they have dinner on the ping-pong table and it keeps collapsing and they make popcorn…" Andie's departure dinner has the same resonance. It is punctuated by tears, but the aim is perhaps the most ambitious throughout Seasons III and IV, to reunite the gang in friendship. Andie reminds them that though Jen had the drugs, she took them of her own free will, thus, they could stop blaming Jen. She then adds: "…Your lives in Capeside are almost over, do you really want them to end this way? Because the only ones who can decide that are sitting at this table. When I first met you… I didn't know much about friendship... or love. Each of you taught me a lot about both. And maybe by leaving... I can return the favor."

And she does help the rifts to heal – that's Andie down to a tee, successful in most things. She had some dangerous scrapes, physical and emotional, but managed to emerge from the other side a teenager who got into Harvard but, equally as important, learned lessons that will make her a more complete person. Her return to Capeside following her sojourn in Italy is the triumphant one she deserved the first time. She is ebullient and effortlessly beautiful. Instead of looking at her trials like the foolish antics of a wayward teen, in retrospect, we can see that they were hurdles Andie had to clear in order to progress as a person. And progressed she has, without a doubt.

Fresh faces

Eve Whitman, Henry Parker, Gretchen Witter, and Drue Valentine may not be major characters in Dawson's Creek but they certainly glide around town as effortlessly as leaves on water. They're protagonists, love interests, sometimes interminable irritations, and though they may not be here to stay, they're certainly indelibly imprinted on the minds of the Capeside clique – and us.

EVE WHITMAN
Played by Brittany Daniel

Could there be a more appropriate name for the temptress of our Adam, better known as Dawson? More often than not, Eve's attire is little more than a few well-placed fig-leaves. But that's her appeal! At least, it is to Dawson, an adolescent boy who laments that he's not a virgin, but whatever comes before virgin. It is probably also her appeal to male fans of the show who were less than impressed with Dawson's efforts to get it on with Eve. There have been few characters like Eve, who could split *Dawson's Creek*'s audience between the sexes. Girls tend not to like her, the lads can do nothing *but* like her.

Eve's a delight to lads. She's not at all fazed by his revelation: "All you are to me is...sex." Make no mistake. She meant business. Girls may side with Joey, who attempted to dismiss Eve as a "bleached blonde ho bag" but she was plenty liked in town. It was not only Pacey who could appreciate Eve's attempts to deflower his virginal friend. Though she tried, Dawson had his reasons for resisting: "… when I sleep with someone for the first time, I don't want it to be for just any reason. I want it to be for every reason." Girls watching sighed in admiration. Guys merely groaned.

One got the sense that others in town admired the way Eve carried herself: confident, articulate, sexy. She waltzed around Capeside High as if she owned the place. And she raised Dawson's credibility countless points when they were caught canoodling in front of an auditorium full of hormonal teenagers. Even though Principal Skinner spotted the girl, he never followed up an investigation into who she was exactly.

Like a cat-burglar she prowled – only to be caught by an ever-vigilant Dawson – snooping around Grams and Jen's property. After playing detective, the Leery lad managed to drag her adoption story from her. Even he had to admit that

Eve to Dawson: (when he gawps at her on a Capeside-bound bus) **"You're drooling."**

"once you get past the lying and the stealing" there was a girl with a heart to be found. She confessed to understanding his relationship with Joey. She had a "boy next door" who, unfortunately was her adoptive father's dad's commanding officer on the army base – cue her exit.

The thought of her traveling up and down the coast seeking her birth mother endeared her to Dawson even more. And, ironically, for all the whimsical behaviour Eve induced in Dawson – semi-nude boat crashes, fund-raising strip parties, SAT test temptation – it was his solid dependency that she relied upon once the secret was out. It was unfortunate she pulled a disappearing act when she did. But of course, that's the delight in Eve; you never know when she may turn up again.

GRETCHEN WITTER
Played by Sasha Alexander

G retchen, like her brother Pacey, thinks it important to try and live up to her surname. She waltzes into town, ousting Pacey from his current spot in Doug's bachelor pad. She attempts to give off the air of a young woman simply taking a break from the pressures of college. But to those of us who know that the first few years of college only pose pressures on your social life, this tale does not ring entirely true.

Gretchen is reluctant to spill the reason for her return to Capeside. She begins working in Leery's Fresh Fish and she and Dawson get close. Where once his crush on her was the kind to simply flatter an older girl and induce sympathy, the warmth between them now is positively invigorating. In time Dawson – as ever the confidant of women – manages to make her feel comfortable enough to relate the real reason she left college.

It is Pacey though, who sees the "world-class jerk" of a boyfriend Nick first hand, when they journey to collect Gretchen's car. Pacey pains for his sis when he learns that unbeknown to atrocious Nick, Gretchen fell pregnant and miscarried, hence her departure from college. Pacey is a little peeved that Gretchen confided in Dawson before him, but Gretchen knows how to deal with the Witter pride, considering she totes a bundle of it around herself.

It is pride that prevents Gretchen from following her gut instinct when she and Dawson share a mistletoe kiss. It is pride that Gretchen has to overcome to keep her stripling relationship alive. The way Pacey laments that Dawson appears to haunt his relationship with Joey mirrors the way Gretchen feels that Joey haunts her relationship with Dawson. There are countless times when Joey has stormed off and Gretchen is left on the sidelines while Dawson pursues to ensure Joey is all right. Never would Gretchen – a witty, charming, knowledgeable young woman – think she would have to compete with a high-school girl. But then again, never would Gretchen have thought she would fall head over common sense in love with a lad who would giggle as he threw water balloons at her.

Gretchen to ex-boyfriend Nick:

"I'm not gonna come upstairs and look at your etchings, so don't ask."

Eve taught Dawson that he could be attracted to a female other than Joey – and that it was okay. Gretchen taught him something more – that he could fall in love with someone other than Joey. Another important lesson that Gretchen imparted was that, even though he was an anxious and impatient teenager, Dawson was not ready to have sex until he felt comfortable discussing it. When he met her friends Keira and Jessica, Dawson – even though he's worldly wise in other areas – was more than a little stunned. Their sexual banter made his brow furrow and the knowledge of how many partners Gretchen had had was perhaps something he did not yet need to know.

Unfortunately, much as Dawson provided succor for her much-bruised emotions, Gretchen had to move on and return to her studies. At the high-school prom, she cannot help but reveal to her little brother: "I never felt pathetic until tonight," after all, here she is at a senior prom all over again. Unable to say goodbye face to face, she leaves a note that Dawson will treasure and the promise that they will meet again as friends in the future.

DRUE VALENTINE
Played by Mark Matkevich

When Gretchen enquires just who the heck this irritating Drue Valentine is, Dawson replies: "You ever meet Abby Morgan?" Drue Valentine is indeed Abby Morgan's clone, except with male attachments. For those of you new to the Creek, Abby was the gang's Iago during Seasons I and II. She delighted in gossip, lies, and viciously accurate put-downs, plainly cast from the same mold as Drue. But like Abby, periodically we get insights into the pain behind the pranks, though they're rare occurrences. There are those who feel Drue is a poor substitute for Chris Wolfe. Indeed, when Chris and Abby got together, they were a formidable foe.

Drue's arrival instantly put Joey on edge. He imitated a wealthy Capeside Yacht Club member and proceeded to rip into everyone who caught his eye. One lady in particular caught his withering sarcasm in thick doses. Joey was shocked when Drue revealed himself to be a lad who intensely disliked his surroundings... and his mother! Dragged from the site of the more rotten delightful distractions of New York to Small Town, USA, what could Drue do but entertain himself with the oh-so-introspective Capeside clique? He was beside himself with glee once he learned that his one-time indiscretion Jen Lindley had made boring Capeside her new home.

Like Abby, Drue couldn't take a hint, no matter how clearly it was made. And Jen clearly told Drue to "curl up and die". Despite this, he would shower Jen with unwanted attention and gifts, namely the Ecstasy that Andie got a hold of. His lack of remorse is legendary. Drue's little pranks – from irritating Dawson, Pacey, and Joey by comparing them to Luke Skywalker, Han Solo, and Princess Leia, to rigging the votes in the senior yearbook – all left a bitter aftertaste.

But of course, he had to get his comeuppance. Dawson, Pacey, and Jack pull a stunning senior stunt by placing Principal Peskin's sailboat and dog, Chester, in the school pool. Better yet, they manage to set up Drue as the most likely suspect, and he gets suspended.

But it's when we see Drue's soft underbelly that we hazard a guess he may not be rotten to the core. Though he lashes out at his date Anna, Joey's dissects him carefully: "This whole witty Drue routine you do, it's just a front for some really scared kid that's desperate for people to love him." He comes clean about his inexperience with women, and we finally see a warm side to his personality. But give him a chance, and he'll steal a kiss, as Joey discovers when they're trapped in the yacht club's storage room. He gets the punch he deserves. Drue claims not to have looked down a sleeping Joey's blouse, but remember, he's an opportunist. Transpires that the poor lad was willing to starve himself (and Joey) simply to escape an unwanted trip to see his estranged father. What can you do but admire someone with as much personality, chutzpah, and wit? Perhaps spare a thought for the troubles which cause him to continually act out.

Wave Makers: Dawson's Creek's Creators

The crew of **Dawson's Creek** are the people we could sit next to on a plane (if we flew business class!) and never know who they were unless a conversation began. Though creator of the show, Kevin Williamson, is no longer involved with the project, the crew have helped the characters he created reach an even wider audience. To sum up the role of the people who work in the background, check out something Pacey said when he applauded Andie for her work on the play (Episode # 313, **Northern Lights**): "I think we both know who the real star is. I mean actors... we just walk on at the last second and grab all the glory, whereas the people behind the scenes – the ones who really make things happen – nobody ever knows about all the hard work they did."

PAUL STUPIN
Executive Producer

Born and raised in California, 39-year-old Paul has never been far from the television and filmmaking hubbub of Hollywood. He studied English at Williams College in Massachusetts, and some of his earlier jobs included tour guide at Universal Studios, page at NBC, and Production assistant on a few other television shows. Though *Dawson's Creek* has been continually on an upward curve since it started, Paul is not resting on his laurels. He continues to have ambitions to, "keep it fresh, exciting, and unpredictable. Something I hope our fans will enjoy for years to come."

What do you do, exactly?

Along with many others, I help to guide the show from every aspect of pre-produc-tion to the final product you see on the air. This includes numerous responsibilities such as sitting in on story meetings, casting, being on the set, going over budget issues, overseeing editing, and even helping with the music on the show. Just choosing it, not composing it.

How did you first meet Kevin Williamson?

I read an early draft of Scream *and fell in love with the wit and the quality of the writing. I was convinced he would be capable of taking a youthful ensemble drama to the next level, so I badgered his agent into a meeting with Kevin and we sat down and started developing* Dawson's Creek *together.*

When the show first aired in 1997, Michael Krantz wrote in *Time* magazine, "Williamson's kids may talk like therapists but they act like guarded and wounded 15-year-olds..." Do you think that was ever an apt description, and is it apt now?

Well, our characters have always been very articulate and particularly adept at expressing themselves. But one thing we have always tried to do is make sure that the emotions and feelings they express are indicative of feelings we have all probably gone through. Our characters feel the same things we all do, they are just better at expressing them.

Honestly – how did the idea of *Dawson's Creek* first strike you?

Honestly, I loved it! The characters and the environment were fresh and exciting and I was immediately curious to see how these fictional lives would unfold. And I think Joey Potter is as interesting today as she was when Kevin first described her.

Explain what you believe is the appeal of the show to teenagers?

Of course, a great deal of the appeal to teenagers has to do with our talented young cast of actors. But I also like to think our show explores certain universal issues and

key points in life to which our viewers of all
ages can relate. If you are fortunate enough to
be able to combine clever and interesting
stories with talented young actors, you're going
to greatly increase your chance for success.

What TV shows did you watch as a teenager?

Growing up, a couple of my favourite shows
were James at 16 as well as Family. I have also
always been sort of a science-fiction geek so I
watched shows like Voyage to the Bottom of
the Sea, Time Tunnel, and all the original
episodes of Star Trek. Of course, I'm being
biased, but I think Dawson's Creek is the best
series ever. I think what separates Dawson's
Creek from the shows I grew up with is that
we are now able to deal with contemporary
issues in an honest and straightforward way –
issues that television shows of the past may
have tried to steer away from.

Are there ever story meetings where the constraints of producing a TV show for teens becomes an issue? Are you ever limited in what stories you would like to write?

Not really. We don't like to regard the show
as just for teens. When we are breaking stories,
we never try to speak down to our audience.
We believe intelligent drama is intelligent
drama – for everyone.

Do you think *Dawson's Creek* could or would ever utilize ideas fans come up with?

Our writers' assistants will tell you that we receive A LOT of email through the
show's website. Believe it or not, we try to read them all. We love to keep in touch
with what our audience thinks, and how they respond to our characters and storylines. But to be honest, I think Dawson's Creek is a very difficult show to write for,
so we try to leave that to our writing staff.

Would you agree the show raises issues that teenagers might feel uncomfortable watching in front of their parents – but are glad to see teens discussing?

Yes, I definitely think so. I'm humbled to say we have often received letters and
emails from parents and young adults who have watched the show together,
telling us about a certain episode that helped open the doors of communication in
their relationship.

Have any interesting press articles about the topics you have covered, made you look at *Dawson's Creek* in a new light?

A lot of research goes into each topic we might discuss in an episode. Also, The Media Project is a non-profit organization that has been very helpful in providing us with information on the health and sex issues we have covered. We try to keep in touch with whatever current issues our audience may be talking about, so when a press article comes out about a certain subject we have already covered, it rarely takes us by surprise. We have in the past received mail from experts in a certain field about a matter we may have covered, who offer their opinions, both good and bad.

Why do you think a significant amount of adults also watch *Dawson's Creek*?

I think there are certain milestones in people's lives that will stay with them into adulthood. Like I said before, certain events and emotions in one's life strike a familiar chord, no matter what the age. Whether it be an older person reminiscing about a similar experience, or a younger person looking forward to that experience. In the end, I think what it comes down to is just interesting storytelling.

Why do you think *Dawson's Creek* is as successful as it is, season after season?

Well, I think we're fortunate in the fact that we were able to establish a very loyal fan base in our first year and we have been building on that each season. But again, a big part of what keeps the viewers coming back year after year is our talented cast and crew.

How early was the decision made to use the Internet? How important is it?

We actually had the idea for the website before the first episode even aired. We knew we would have a very internet-savvy audience, and wanted to create a site that went deeper than most other show sites. One that allows our fans to delve deeper into the world of Dawson's Creek, rather than just giving you a recount of certain facts that you may already know. It has become an integral part of the show because our audience often uses it as a sounding board, and we use it to see what they are thinking.

How do you respond to criticism that kids DO NOT talk like that?

We never intended the way our characters speak to be indicative of the real world. They speak in a very articulate and idealized way, in a manner in which many of us wish we could express ourselves, whether as teenagers or adults. I think it plays a big part in the appeal of the show and is what keeps Dawson's Creek unique and special. These kids may be great talkers, but they are still as confused and challenged by the same issues as we all are.

What has been your favourite on-screen moment of the show?

Without a doubt, the now famous kiss between Dawson and Joey at the end of Season I and beginning of Season II.

What about your favourite off-screen moment? Has anything happened that had the crew cracking up that hasn't made it past the editing suite?

Well, I would have to say my favourite off-screen moments have been weekends down in Wilmington when the cast and crew get together on an island to barbecue and goof around on the beach. A funny moment on the set in recent memory occurred during the filming of Episode #410, The Tao of Dawson. The scene called for Dawson to come across a sleeping Mr Brooks, played by Harve Presnell, and lay a blanket over him. The camera started rolling, and as James approached, he revealed he was carrying a pillow instead, and proceeded to mock-smother Harve. We didn't see it until later, but it was quite amusing.

How often do you read the emails that are sent to the website? Can you recall a memorable one?

We read our emails constantly because we like to see what our audience is thinking and what they are talking about. Some of our writers and assistants have actually been known to go inside Dawson's Creek chat rooms after a new episode has shown, to get the fans' reactions! Over the past season we have received a lot of interesting gifts in the office from the fans.

How can you see the characters progressing?

Well, I don't want to give away too much about the upcoming year, but I will say that with all of our characters entering college and uprooting to new towns, it should make for quite an interesting season.

Why couldn't Dawson handle Eve?

That's a tough one. I don't know too many high-school boys who could've handled a beautiful, nomadic, grifting stripper. I know I couldn't have.

Any amusing anecdotes you can add?

Well, I think that viewers would be interested to know that the "Would You Rather" game Dawson, Joey, Jen, and Jack are seen playing on the finale of Season IV, was actually a real-life game the writers, assistants, and I would play in the office.

GREG PRANGE
Co-Executive Producer

The Detroit, Michigan native now resides in both Los Angeles and Wilmington, North Carolina, where *Dawson's Creek* is filmed. Married with three boys aged 22, 20 and 14, Greg has a real insight into the minds of a large portion of the viewing audience. To date, Greg has worked on five series, six features, five pilots and 35 Movies of the Week.

But his ambitions are still burning bright and where *Dawson's Creek* is concerned, Greg would like to "continue making an honest and thoughtful show."

What do you do exactly?

There are 3 executive producers on this series and we all have somewhat different responsibilities. I am primarily located in Wilmington and handle the shooting phase of the show. As well as directing some of the episodes, I am in charge of the day-to-day operation of the filming. I think the most important part of my job though is to hire the right people to work with.

How did you first meet Kevin Williamson, *Dawson's Creek* creator?

They had originally shot a 30-minute presentation of the show. I was not involved in the presentation, but when it went on to be created into a series, Kevin and Paul Stupin hired me to produce it.

When the show first aired in 1997, Michael Krantz wrote in *Time* Magazine: "Williamson's kids may talk like therapists but they act like guarded and wounded 15-year-olds..." Do you think that was ever an apt description, and is it apt now?

I think that although our characters did and do talk in an idealized type of speech, they were and are still just teenagers trying to explore the elements of growing up. There are so many phases that young people go through in their teenage years and hopefully we are just trying to respond to the emotions they go through.

Honestly – how did the idea of *Dawson's Creek* first strike you?

After the presentation had been made, it was one of the new series that I (thankfully) was up for. I looked at the pilot and told my wife that this was a show I would like to be associated with. Five years later I still feel the same way.

Explain what you believe is the appeal of the show to teenagers?

I think it is a show about them that does not talk down to them. I believe people of most ages can find things in these characters we can relate to.

Are there ever script meetings where the constraints of producing TV for teenagers becomes an issue?

Though I am not primarily involved in the writing phase of the show, I still have to be responsive to the needs of the script and the needs of the network. Since it is television and there are constraints on what you can portray to the audience, I still feel we are given a lot of creative freedom to explore growing up in today's society. In some ways, since we can't be quite as loose as feature films, I think it makes us a little more sensitive to how we portray things.

Did you know that Star Trek invites scripts from fans and will utilize ideas they come up with? Do you think _Dawson's Creek_ could or would ever do that – the show receives a lot of email after all.

I think we all try to keep up with what the audience thinks and respond to, but in a serialized drama it would be hard to change course based upon email input. But you never know when Paul Stupin may even surprise me.

Would you agree that the show raises issues that teenagers might feel uncomfortable watching in front of their parents – but are glad to see teens discussing?

I don't know if I agree with that. I have teenagers and a lot of their friends watch the show and when I talked to their parents they seem as up on it as the kids. I think the key is to raise issues to be talked about.

Why do you think a significant amount of adults also watch it?

Because I think it is a show about people and how people react to each other. We frame it in the teenage years, but feelings and insecurities and joy happen to us all throughout life.

There have been other teen soaps, _Beverly Hills 90210_, _My So Called Life_ and even docudrama like MTV's _Real World_ – why do you think _Dawson's Creek_ is as successful as it is, season after season?

I think all these other shows have made their imprint on the culture and I believe we continue to do that as well. Truth, Justice, and the human way (blah, blah, blah!) But really, quality writing and an incredible cast. I think a lot of the audience has grown up with us.

How do you respond to the criticism that kids DO NOT talk like that?

I think they do, sometimes we just don't listen. You know I can't talk like that either, but I can feel like that.

Your favourite off-screen moment of the show?

Since we have filmed for about 575 days now, it is hard to pull a moment that would be my favourite. But if I were pressed, it would have to be during Episode #412 ... the water was freezing cold and our first assistant cameraman Frank Godwin took a bet and swam across the channel and back in the middle of the night. We have it on tape to prove it too!

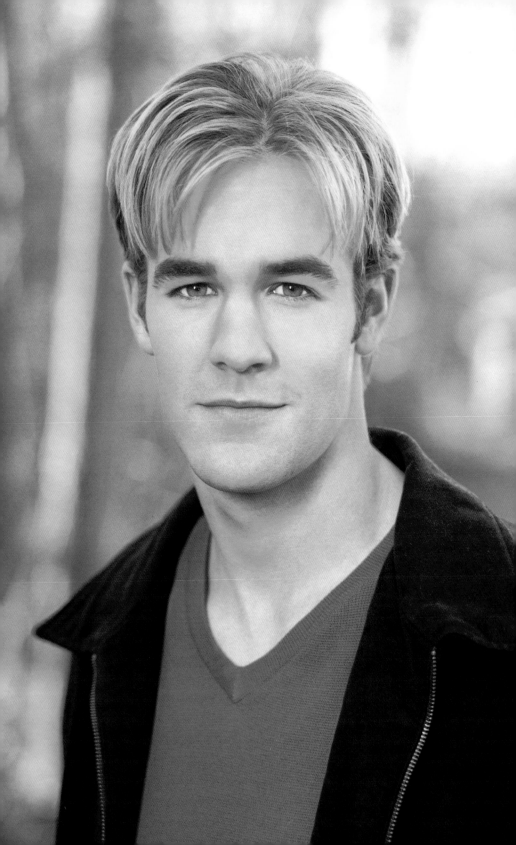

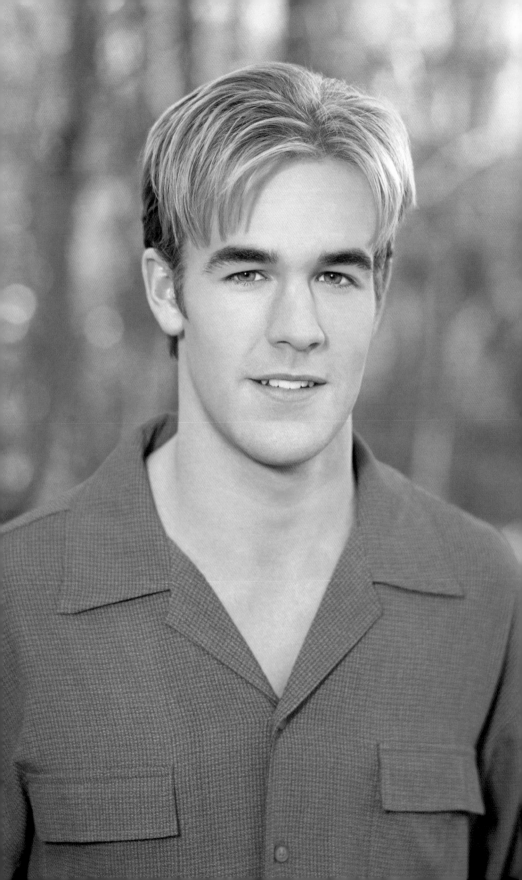

How often do you read the emails that are sent to the website? How do they affect you? Can you recall a memorable one?

I don't read them very often. I always seem to have too much to do in too little time! I try not to take it personally, because sometimes they are quite ill spirited, but if everybody liked everything that would mean you are not pressing hard enough.

What is your take on the characters – and how can you see them progressing?

Suffice it too say that wherever these characters head in life, it will be with passion, angst, conviction, and oh did I mention angst?

GREG BERLANTI
Executive Producer

Born in Suffern, New York, Greg, 29, grew up in New York State but now lives in the Hollywood Hills, California. He studied theater at Northwestern University and insists he had, "over 100 of the worst temp jobs out there" before landing his current post. His future ambitions for the show include participating in its continuing success.

What do you do, exactly?

On a day-to-day basis, things change constantly so that's difficult to answer. But if we're looking at the big picture, my primary focus is to work on creating good story-lines, then reworking them and rewriting them to make sure we put the best possible show on air.

How is it that different writers keep the flavor of the show the same?

The characters that Kevin Williamson created have a very distinct voice, which we try to maintain. And when in doubt, we go back to who they were in the beginning.

Star Trek invites scripts from fans and will utilize ideas they come up with. Do you think Dawson's Creek would ever do that?

No, I don't think the show could or would do that because shows like Star Trek aren't serialized in the way ours is. We set up character and plot points way in advance, which makes our audience months and months behind us. So, you see this isn't possible. That said, we do like to give young writers an opportunity.

Honestly – how did the idea of Dawson's Creek first strike you?

The first season when I wasn't on the show, I appreciated it's intelligence, vulnerability, and nostalgic tone, but never in a million years did I think I'd be writing it.

Explain what you believe to be the fundamental appeal of the show to teenagers?

I think the appeal of the show to everyone, not just teens, is that our characters are very self-aware, very intelligent, and say everything we would say after thinking about it for 20 minutes. But they are still wide eyed and innocent in their own way.

What television shows did you watch as a teenager? Explain them a little – how different are they to what is on television today for teenagers?

I didn't watch teen shows. I tended to watch more adult shows when I was growing up, like L.A. Law and thirtysomething. I would say that, what is so great about Dawson's Creek *is that it deals with very adult issues.*

Has there been any press coverage that made you ponder the issues *Dawson's Creek* covers?

One of our proudest moments here was when Newsweek *cited Jack's first kiss as a pinnacle in TV history. It reminded us of the impact we all have.*

Why do you think a significant amount of adults also watch the show?

It reminds them of their youth and their struggle to become who they are now.

What do you think has made the series grow from the pilot to Season IV?

Across the board, really wonderful writing, directing, and acting. Everyone has grown with the show and that's helped keep it really strong and fresh.

There have been other teen soaps, *Beverly Hills 90210*, *My So Called Life* and even docudrama like MTV's *Real World* – why do you think *Dawson's Creek* is as successful as it is, season after season?

Because it's sort of a combination of those shows. It has the timeliness of 90210, *the solid writing of* My So Called Life, *and it really blends all those shows together at their best.*

How do you respond to the criticism that kids DO NOT talk like that?

Maybe they don't, but they wish they could.

What has been your favourite on-screen moment of the show?

Jack's coming out.

How can you see the characters progressing?

We've entered the college years, and their small world will start to broaden, but the question remains – will their friendships endure?

JOHN McCULLOUGH
Music Supervisor

Born in Canada, *Dawson Creek's* music supervisor now lives in Los Angeles. He studied music at various universities and his early jobs included being an orchestral and session player. His future ambitions for the show include continuing to discover and feature new music that will "enhance the stories".

What do you do, exactly?
I seek out music that can be considered for the series and suggest music to the editors and Paul Stupin, Executive Producer. I also assist in obtaining the rights to include the music in the series. Bottom line is, I listen to a lot of music!

Why do you think the music is SO important to the show?
The music assists in setting the tone or mood for a scene and in heightening the emotion of our stories and characters.

The show could have featured no modern music, why go for the method of sourcing new music every week?
We like to discover unknown great songs and talent.

Who chooses the songs?
It's a truly collaborative effort involving everyone who works on the show. However, the final decision is down to the Executive Producer, Paul Stupin.

However do you begin to match the plethora of emotions with music?
Typically, we will try a lot of different songs for a very emotional scene and just keep listening until we find the right one.

Joey once warned Dawson about looking for deep meanings in popular song lyrics – what's your take on that?
Every listener/viewer will have a different reaction to a song lyric. This is what makes music so special.

The internet allows people to make suggestions – do you ever follow them up?
Yes, all the time. We are fortunate to have a fantastic music website which is run by Craig Bricker. Craig forwards me the suggestions to think about.

Do any unsigned bands have their music included?
About 50 percent of the songs we use come from what we call indie or unsigned bands.

Dawson's Creek on the Internet

Dawson, Joey, Pacey, Jen, Jack, and Andie are most definitely kids of the digital age. Remember Dawson filming the Potter Bed-and-Breakfast to create a virtual tour on the web? Or Jack exchanging emails with a cowardly Henry Parker who wanted to end his relationship with Jen? Well, these are the ways the creators of the show have reminded us how much technology has changed our lives. Here we speak to the people responsible for turning Dawson's Creek into such a rich online environment.

Dawson's Creek has always had an internet-aware audience. A variety of sites has been created that allow fans to research, discuss, and explore the boundaries of the weekly show. However, Sony were able to elevate this experience to previously unheard of levels. The original premise of Dawson's Desktop – being able to peek through Dawson's computer – has expanded into one of the largest, richest, most satisfying online environments ever created.

In the online arena, Dawson's Creek and its affiliated sites have maintained their position in the game through constant evolution. A close partnership between the writers of the show and the creators of the website has meant a seamless coordination of up-to-the-minute storylines. Even when the show is not on air, fans can keep abreast of what the characters are up to through Dawson's Desktop. If only the Waltons had had such opportunities open to them!

Sony Pictures Digital Entertainment has made strides in programming and presentation. Even though the current variety of Dawson's Creek-related sites include chat rooms, homepages, music links, the desktops, message boards, Capeside.net, and the various character homepages, if the fans keep logging on, the sites will keep expanding.

CHRIS PIKE
Director of Development,
Sony Pictures Digital Entertainment

Born in Leavenworth, Kansas and raised in "the lovely San Fernando Valley", Chris Pike studied radio, television and film at university and began working at AND Communications upon graduating. He has now been with Sony for seven years, first with Columbia TriStar Interactive and for the past year and a half with SPDE. When Dawson's Desktop was developed, Chris was responsible for the entire Columbia TriStar Television website (20-plus shows). He coordinated the sites for shows such as *Party of Five, Mad About You*, and *V.I.P.* He now lives in Mar Vista, California with his wife and twin baby girls.

What do you do, exactly?
I create original online shows, based on ideas I come up with, other Sony properties, and ideas sent my way. It's my job to take an idea and make it work online to keep users interested and coming back week after week.

How do you seamlessly integrate the television and online experiences?
On Dawson's Desktop we focus on the core story elements. We're sent these in advance by the show and we then weave a creative online arch, which teases, but doesn't give away, key elements of the on-air story.

Are there any advantages in working in an online environment as opposed to the televisual?
One of the advantages for the audience is that they don't have to be held to the

traditional "viewing by appointment" theory of standard network television. They can experience the story anytime they desire, and because we constantly update the site, the experience is always fresh.

From a production viewpoint, an advantage would be that our "episodes" consist of a week's worth of content – much of it written in the character's voice – we have the ability to spend more time with the characters on a deeper level then you can within the confines of a weekly episode.

How have the dawsonscreek.com website and Dawson's Desktop websites developed over recent years?

One of the things I am most proud of is the way we've continually adapted the web experience for our users to keep up with the creative direction of the series. We try really hard to push ourselves to evolve the user's experience and keep it a fresh and vital part of their enjoyment of the show.

The Desktop was originally launched with the simple premise of allowing users to view the life of main character Dawson Leery via his home computer. This metaphor allowed us to tell the story of his life 24 hours a day, seven-days a week, and thus give fans the ultimate immersion in the Dawson's Creek experience.

One of the first early challenges we faced was how to keep the story going when the show ended its run for the year. Luckily we received unparalleled cooperation from the show's executive producer Paul Stupin, and were able to create an authorized fictional account of Dawson's summer vacations spent in Philadelphia with his mom.

This season we took the risky gamble of rotating the Desktops between the characters Dawson, Joey, Pacey, and Jen. Instead of just telling our story from one point of view, we could shift to better address the character whose narrative seemed most to be driving the story. Luckily this gamble paid off, handsomely, and we attracted the best traffic numbers ever.

This summer we launched the Dawson's Creek *Summer Diaries*, a unique way for users to follow their favorite character all summer long. This year's version of the "diaries" will feature cool user participation.

As for next season, what with the kids going off to college and a new location, we are in the process of looking into ways to update the experience. It's too early to be sure, but I can safely say that we'll find a way for users to keep track of all the characters on a weekly basis.

What do you think about fan websites?

On the whole we love fan sites. One of the ways we convinced the studio to fund Desktop was by showing them the passionate following online – we felt this would assure the success of our project. The only time we feel less than love is on the rare occasion they show full-length episodes, which becomes a legal issue. Then we need to practice "tough love"!

How do you aim to maintain interest in the show when new episodes are not airing at the time?

We hope that the fans in some small way consider the Desktop as a true extension of the character's universe and thus remain interested in the opportunity to follow the story no matter what the network schedule permits.

Why was it felt necessary to create a distinct site for the music of *Dawson's Creek*, dawsonscreekmusic.com?

We wanted to keep the non-corporate feel of this tremendous fan site and felt it would be best accomplished by not folding into our site.

How successful has this site been?

This site has been a major success with fans and a helpful device for the show's producers to give bands the special attention they deserve, as music is such a focal point of the show.

The chat rooms, homepages, music links, desktops, message boards, Capeside High site, and the whole virtual Capeside.net sites add up to a colossal online experience – any further plans to extend the site?

We're always planning new things and new ways to extend the Dawson's Creek universe. If the fans keep coming we'll keep building up the site.

ARIKA MITTMAN
Producer, Dawson's Desktop

Born and raised in Long Island, New York, Arika now lives in Santa Monica, California. The 27-year-old studied English and Theater at Wesleyan University in Connecticut. Arika at first worked in casting and then began work in production. Some of the other shows she has worked on include teen drama *Beverley Hills 90210*, the soap operas *Days of Our Lives*, *General Hospital*, *The Young and the Restless* and a pilot called *Wind on Water*. Her connection with

Dawson's Creek has grown as time has gone on. She was a writer's assistant for two years before moving into producing the Desktop series. Her future ambitions for the show are centered on how interesting the characters' college years will be. "There are so many exciting things to do these next few years!"

What do you do, exactly?

I produce the Dawson's Creek Desktops – which basically means I'm in charge of all the writing on the site, including everything from the emails the characters exchange to the Summer Diaries, as well as all the character updates and episode guides you see on dawsonscreek.com. I don't do the programming – which is a good thing, since I don't even know HTML! I supervise all the creative elements of the site including the design, and I'm also the "editor in chief" of Capenet!

When we first spoke some years ago you said: "I had never done anything for online publications before..." how does it feel now, a few years down the line, producing the desktops?

I've learned a lot since that time! I've become quite a bit more comfortable with this medium. In fact, I recently worked with Paul Stupin on a new online series for Sony called "Rachel's Room," on which I served as head writer. It's been very rewarding seeing the popularity of the Desktops increase over the course of the seasons.

Dawson's Desktop was originally meant as a publicity tool for the show but it has taken on a life of its own – describe how things developed over recent years.

The Desktops were originally designed to publicize the show... but the amount of visitor traffic it received proved that the Desktop was really holding its own. And when that traffic held steady through the summer thanks to the Summer Diaries, it became very clear that the online extension is an integral part of the show. Dawson's Desktop has served as a model for Sony as we expand to create more original online entertainment.

How do you aim to maintain interest in the show when new episodes are not on air?

Last summer, we did the Summer Diaries. They kept the users up to date on what Jen, Dawson, Andie, and Jack were up to in Capeside, and on what Joey and Pacey were experiencing during their summer aboard Pacey's boat. That feature was so popular that we really had to challenge ourselves to improve upon it. With that in mind, we are launching the Summer To Remember this year, which will incorporate summer diaries for all the characters, and in addition, will allow users to keep their own diaries, and to take part in the Summer Surveys alongside their favorite characters. We also launched the Capeside High Online Yearbook in May, and expect that will continue to grow and hold users' interest over the summer.

Can you describe the actual writing production process for Dawson's Desktop: how does what is happening on the show, for example, affect what is happening on the websites?

We stay very closely connected with the show. We do our best to drop little hints about what's to come on the show, and we expand upon the elements of the show that don't make it into the one hour per week that the show covers.

Do you feel you have more freedom on the Desktop to explore the characters' minds?

Definitely. The show is the external world of the characters – you're viewing it from the outside. On the Desktops, you're on the inside. It's an internally oriented rather than an externally oriented experience.

The characters are certainly more risqué online than they would be on television – is this a deliberate move?

I don't think we set out to be more risqué. In some ways we are less, since it's mostly text, so there's not much to actually see. But we definitely aren't as constricted by network broadcast standards, which does give us some additional freedom. But we do have to be responsible. We limit the language the same way that it is limited on the show. I think that because of the intimate nature of the Desktops and private journals, it feels more risqué because you're reading things that are so personal and private. But we're not looking for shock value. We're simply staying honest, real, and true to the characters.

How have you developed the storylines involving "online characters" such as Dawson's cousins Brad and his sister Amanda – folks we have never seen on screen?

The arcs of these characters have been developed only online, which means that their stories are told entirely through emails, instant messages, and journal entries. It seems strange at first, but through the correspondence, we're able to develop the characters and plots without the traditional "narration." Our audience is very bright; they pick up on it. They understand what's going on without having it spoon-fed to them.

Aunt Gillian is creepy! Please explain who she is and where she gets her powers!

She's not that creepy! She's Gale's other sister, besides the one you saw on TV, Aunt Gwen. While Aunt Gwen is the hippie, Aunt Gillian is the New Age experimenter. She has studied everything from astrology to Tarot cards to crystals. While Aunt Gillian might come across as something of a "kook" to the family, the astute user might notice she's definitely at least a little bit psychic...

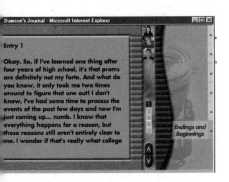

Of all the situations that you have written about, which one do you look back on with most pride?

I would have to say Joey and Pacey's Summer Diaries. It was really exciting to be able to explore their love story in those first special moments – moments that we never got to witness on the show. The fans really loved it, and I really enjoyed writing it.

What are the advantages/disadvantages of the instant email feedback available from fans of the sites?

I guess the fact that they can catch our little mistakes and point them out to us is a bit of a mixed blessing! It's great when we can fix things – like when they catch a typo or an error on a page – but it's hard when we disappoint the fans with inconsistencies. We try very hard to maintain high standards – because when we make mistakes... they notice! But it's fun to watch them dissect and analyze all the little moments we work so hard for. It's great knowing it matters to them. They don't just look at what it says, but at what it means... that's great!

What is the most interesting email you have had from the fans?

Oh boy... we've gotten some very interesting stuff. I don't think I could pick just one. Mostly they tell us which couples they want to be together... What's funny is we often get emails asking if Joey really wrote that email, or just someone pretending to be Joey. I think they forget that a "real" Joey doesn't exist!

Where do you get your ideas from? You obviously have the show as inspiration, but a brave new world has been created online – how do you accomplish this?

We often take our cues from what happens on the show and think of how we can organically expand upon it. In Season III, for instance, Joey's family opened a Bed and Breakfast, and on the show, Dawson said he was creating a Virtual Tour for the web. So we built a whole site for the B&B ostensibly created by Dawson. In addition, at the end of Season IV, with the characters graduating from Capeside High, it was a perfect time to create the Capeside High Online Yearbook! Some ideas come from the world outside; for instance, I've noticed the popularity of "personality tests" on other websites, and thus created a "Dawson's Creek" personality test which determines which DC character you are. Features like that tap into an audience who aren't just visiting Dawsonscreek.com, but who are online all the time.

We constantly challenge ourselves to make the site better. What started as only Dawson's Desktop has this year expanded to The Dawson's Creek Desktops,

including Joey's, Dawson's, Pacey's, and Jen's Desktops, which appear on a rotating basis. As the show has developed, it has become more of an ensemble show, and thus it's become important to bring the other characters into the mix. This allows us to see the world not only from Dawson's perspective... but to get a different character's perspective every week!

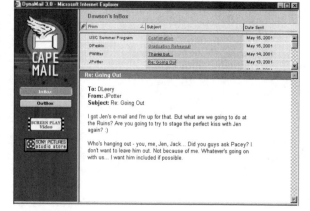

FOR THE NEWCOMERS TO THE SURF

If any of you are new to the world of online activities connected to *Dawson's Creek*, you may also need a little help with the terminology. You are likely to be asked whether you agree with TPTB, or if you are a J/Per. Here, we give you a quick guide so you can surf with the aficionados without being blazed in a hail of burning postings.

Newbie – name given to someone new to a fan forum or discussion board.

Fan Forum – a place where people can post messages, like a public email, that can be read and replied to by others.

Thread – as messages on a topic expand, you can view the 'thread' which is the entire strand of messages from the original post, down to the most recent.

Bash/Blaze/Burn – impolite messages that insult a person who has posted a message that someone does not agree with. Not nice – but sometimes funny to read!

Fan Fiction – budding writers of the show will pen various events for the well-known characters, attempting to speak in their voices. There is a huge amount of fan fiction, a bizarre world where Pacey could still be dating Joey or where even stranger things happen.

Aussie Thread, UK Thread etc – not everyone views the show the same time as it airs in the US. Sometimes other countries could be as much as ten episodes behind, and so people who do not want to spoil the denouement of a storyline may only read threads related to their countries.

TPTB – the powers that be – the creators of the show. Make no mistake, sometimes die-hard fans intensely dislike certain directions the characters take. This is a moment when TPTB are blamed and torn to shreds quite mercilessly. People really care about these characters.

J/Pers – believers in the relationship between Joey and Pacey (the really heartbroken amongst this group don't even like to acknowledge the fact that Pacey and Joey have split up on the show!)

D/Jers – believers in the everlasting "soulmates" status of Dawson and Joey. So if you're in a fan forum and are asked, "Are you a D/Jer or a J/Per", you will understand that someone wants to know where your affiliations lie.

The Bitter Club – people who appreciate Jen and Jack's darker view of love and life. When Jen was dating Henry Parker, this group was left supporting Jack. Now that Jack is dating Tobey, it looks as if single Jen is going to be left carrying the banner for the Bitter Club – at least for a while.

The Unbearable Lightness of Being... A Teenager!

Dawson's Creek *has never been an "issue show" – one that deliberately sets out to tackle a different issue each week. However, the show has still not shied away from dealing with interesting topics during the course of four seasons. If you are a teen and you reside in Capeside, you had better get used to taking the choppy weather along with the smooth. The travails of teen lives have never been so well documented as in* Dawson's Creek *– jobs, colleges, therapy, and, of course, first-time sex.*

WHERE'S THE FUN IN WORKING 4 TILL 8?
It would be nice if the gang could recline by the creek all the time but life is just not that easy – even on television.

Though Dawson has a new jeep and sports snazzy clothes all the time, we suspect, rightly, that these are the gifts of doting parents. After all, Dawson is an only child. But as punishment for getting arrested at a party (Episode #314, *Valentine's Day's Massacre*), Mitch puts his son to work in the fledgling family restaurant. By the sounds of things, Dawson is desperate to get out of it: "Dad, it was a party. And I'm 16." But Mitch is intractable; Dawson will work until he understands that: "… suddenly deciding to be a kid doesn't give you license to be reckless and irresponsible." Dawson turns out to be a great bonus at the restaurant. And the restaurant turns out to be a great bonus for him, not least because he gets to spend time with Gretchen who begins working there when she turns up in town.

Dawson to Mitch:
"I'm trying to get back to the basics of being a kid. And kids have fun and screw up."

Dawson's job at the video store seems to have waned as time goes by, though he was once spotted there (but not with Pacey who had to give up after-

school jobs to make up his grades in extra classes). What shift did Dawson work exactly? Every other full moon? Something Dawson appeared to have done consistently was paint houses all summer long, with Jack. Dawson is one of those gifted youths who can turn his hand to pretty much anything. Thus, when we hear Arthur Brooks griping about the way Dawson is painting his house – to repay for wrecking the Brooks' boat – we know the problem has got to lie with the miserable Brooks. However, only two Capeside residents appear to have ever won Brooks' appreciation – Dawson and Grams. The house painting puts Dawson in touch with a truly talented filmmaker who stepped out of the fast lane following a broken heart. You had better believe Dawson could relate to that, having recently lost the impetus to hold a film camera. It is Brooks that rekindles Dawson's fire for film. Equally as important, it is Brooks that encourages the shy lad to "quit flirting and kiss her already" when he sees him dillydallying with Gretchen underneath the mistletoe.

By far the most hard-working teen in Capeside, Joey has one reason for working every moment she isn't either studying or sleeping. Her motivation is her desire to leave Capeside. She has had the most jobs out of anyone – including Mitch! She has worked at The Ice House, Logan's Marina, and the Capeside Yacht Club. Though it seems she did this unpaid, she can also have been said to work in the new family enterprise, the Potter Bed-and-Breakfast.

The Ice House was one of those small tourist-town restaurants where the banter and food were both pleasant. It was the site of many a teen adventure. Once, when Abby Morgan had pushed too many buttons for Joey's liking, she received a jug of iced water on her head. It was also the place where Joey met the guy who gave her her first kiss. Anderson was a rich young buck on holiday from New York and Joey, smitten, went on a date with him. When the time was right, he kissed her and though she enjoyed it, she threw away his number, realizing that they were perhaps too different and lived too far apart to pursue a relationship. The Ice House was also the place where Joey shared a kiss with Jack, who worked as a waiter there for a while. Trouble was, she was dating Dawson at the time (Episode #205, *Full Moon Rising*). It was with that kiss, though, that Joey realized that though she did love Dawson, she needed something more than him at that moment in time.

By far the most surprising thing that took place at The Ice House though, was Joey's father using it as a drug trafficking den just before it burned down in highly suspicious circumstances. Dawson had discovered this truth before Joey. Imagine the ruminating Dawson went through before challenging Mr Potter thus: "I don't believe that a man who claims to love his children with all his heart and soul would jeopardize their happiness by trafficking cocaine

through the family business." When Joey
eventually learns of her father's betrayal, she
wears a police wire to record an admission from
him. When he gives up the ghost, she says: "I
trusted you. You lied, you ruined everything that
Bessie and I have worked so hard for... We could
have died in that fire, Dad. It would have been
your fault." (Episode #222, *Parental Discretion
Advised.*)

Joey's job at Logan's Marina may not have
been as fraught with parental issues, but it
certainly had its trying co-workers. Rob Logan,
Senator's son, spoilt brat and sexist pig, was
working at his father's business as teach a lesson
for various indiscretions. But it's doubtful Rob
could spell discretion. He had a habit of sneaking
in on Joey just when she happened to be
changing and he asked her repeatedly for a date.
But leave it to Joey to decline with wicked wit:
Rob: "So, whatta you say, Potter? You and me,
movies tonight?" Joey (with a roll of her eyes):
"Oh, joy. Is this the part of our workday where
you get inappropriate?" When he later asks if all
teenage girls are as "uptight" as her, she merely
responds: "No, just the ones with half a brain."
Unfortunately for Joey though, Rob has hiring and
firing powers and fires her as she closed the
marina early in order to crash his date with Andie.
The real reason, as we know, was Joey disliked
him and was not afraid to show this. Big egos dent
easily. After Logan's Marina, came the Capeside
Yacht Club, managed by the banished New York

socialite, Mrs Valentine. Pacey calls her "Satan's handmaiden" (Episode #413,
Hopeless) much to Joey's mirth. But as if the dragon was not enough to contend
with, Joey also has to deal with the worm of New York, Drue Valentine. Though
he saved her butt on the first day (let's forget for a moment that he was the
one who originally got her into trouble) Joey quickly and effortlessly puts him
in his place. He is the lad who sits behind her in class for no other reason
than to pull her hair and bug her. Joey quickly realises that here is a spoilt, only
child who has had his own way for too long and found unorthodox ways of
entertaining himself. Drue is an epicurean of the highest standards. Though Joey
had requested he keep an eye on the weather channel when she suspected
there may be a storm, he gets distracted by Pamela Anderson running about
in *V.I.P.* When the storm rolls in, however, stranding Pacey and Jen in its
tumultuous midst, Drue has to receive some praise for giving Dawson the keys
to Mr Brooks' boat so that he could save the shipwrecked duo. The Capeside
Yacht Club is not Joey's dream job by far, but at least it helped her to support
her sister and her nephew and enabled her to put a little away for college.

The Potter Bed-and-Breakfast meant that Joey's housekeeping duties were extended to include guests. Joey tried her best with *Bed & Breakfast Quarterly*'s snooty reviewer, Fred Fricke, but he was singularly unimpressed – at first. Later, he became aware of the fact that though the boiler was busted, here were two young ladies who knew how to create a home away from home for their guests. And that's the thing with Joey. Many of the places she has worked have been beset by adventure – but she brings her pretty face, wit, and warmth wherever she goes. Capeside's businesses will miss her.

WHAT'S IT LIKE TO SERVE THE COMMUNITY?
Leave it to Jen to get something positive from a negative; in this case meeting a doppelganger while doing community service.

Jen Lindley is a teen who, like Dawson, seems not to worry where the money for her next outfit is coming from. Perhaps her fabulously wealthy dad – overcome with guilt – let her keep a credit card or three when he banished his wayward little girl. And it's more than likely that the dollar goes a little further in Capeside than it does in New York. Although we do not see Jen actually work for a dollar, she is required to put in community service following

Drue's helpful blabber mouth. He informs Mitch that he and Jen participated in Andie's drug-taking. Grams is "utterly disappointed" in Jen but the community service enables her grand-daughter to learn a lot.

While helping Tobey with Responsible Rides (Episode #412, *The Te of Pacey*), an organization that drives drunk teens home, Jen comes across a very aware, very young girl. "I drink red wine and I read Nabokov and I'm not a virgin, okay?" the girl protests, trying to prove her maturity. This strikes a chord with Jen who, as we know, was equally aware and sophisticated at that young girl's age and yet made some mistakes that she later regretted. During the ride home, Jen can hold her tongue no longer and challenges the girl, informing her: "I've had more hangovers, more men, and a lot more time to figure out which roads lead straight to heartache." But the girl doesn't want to hear it – storming out of the van. It is perhaps this incident that puts Jen on the route to therapy, to appease the angry little girl within herself.

HAVE YOU DONE YOUR COLLEGE ESSAYS YET?

Glossy brochures and essays with damned-awful titles like "Why Do You Want To Be A Filmmaker?" must mean it is college application time.

Andie, being the A-type personality that she is, had the whole college application thing under her belt by the time she was about five-and-a-half. Jack, though, needed a little kick from his Tae-Bo sister to get him jump-started. Andie insists he pad out his college application with a little kids' soccer coaching. He's reluctant at first but once he starts forming relationships with the children, especially recalcitrant Molly – who turns out to be an ace in goal – he loves it. Unfortunately, Molly's sister makes a move on Jack. When he tells her he is gay, the news speeds round the soccer parents like a good striker speeds round a goalkeeper. He is later fired, under the pretence that he is no good for the team. He knows it is because he is gay – but he is not too pleased when Tobey blatantly points this out at a Gay-Straight Teen coalition: "The parents fired you when they found out you were queer. Though of course they were very careful not to fire you because you are queer."

It's a tad ironic, then, that Tobey recommends Jack's next job. Jack's a little reluctant at first saying: "I'm not interested in a repeat of the soccer incident" but the volunteer reading programme is perfect for Jack, and he proves to be very skilled. Unfortunately, Tobey's advances mean Jack considers not turning up. "Whatever it is that attracts two people, we don't have it. It's no one's fault" Tobey is heartbroken leading Jack to add: "Maybe it's not a good idea for us to do this tutoring thing together." But they both realize that it is supposed to be for the children's benefit and thus manage to put their feelings behind them.

It transpires that Jack is so good at college applications that Grams uses his skills to ensure Jen completes hers. Following Andie's trials and errors with illegal drugs, Grams withdrew all kind of friendship from Jen. She, in turn, withdrew into herself, feeling that no-one cared about her. She felt it was pointless going to college as there would be no-one to congratulate or commiserate with her. She spits at Grams that she can no longer discuss her future with her: "You lost that right when you wrote me off." (Episode #409, *Kiss Kiss, Bang Bang*) Grams realizes it is time to capitulate and she seeks Jack's excellent assistance. He writes Jen's essays with the damned-awful titles and ensures they are in on time to Ms Watson, the college application co-ordinator. When Jen discovers this, she is furious but calms down when she realizes the sacrifice that Grams is willing to make in order to educate her. In the end, both Jack and Jen get accepted by most of the colleges they applied to.

Joey's acceptance by Worthington posed a problem however; the university reckoned Bessie could afford to fund a significant proportion of the cost. Joey was completely heartbroken, collapsing in tears at the thought of her dreams, so nearly grasped, slipping away from her like an eel into the creek. What made the blow all the heavier was that all her efforts, both in school and after school in the workplace, seemed to amount to nothing. When it came down to it, she was just a poor girl from the wrong side of the creek who could not afford to go to university, despite possessing intelligence quite a few college grads would be proud to have. Even though Dawson offers the money with no hesitation, Joey's pride – and her worry that the money would cause further irreparable damage to her and Dawson's relationship – means she cannot accept it. Dawson says though: "If our friendship could survive last summer, then it can survive anything." He adds: "All the pain I've watched you go through – I've never been able to fix it before. But this I can fix. All I'm asking you to do is let me." Although Pacey shares some of Joey's concerns, he knows that Joey will not be happy anywhere else and persuades her to accept the money, which she does. Joey's acceptance of the money heralds more than the start of her college education. It is her admittance that she needs help – like all of us sometimes – and that it is not wrong to take it when offered by true friends.

Was there really ever any doubt that Dawson would not go to a prestigious university to study film? Well, there was actually. Following his break-up with Joey, Dawson fell into a film funk. Movie night was a sporadic instead of a regular affair. The fiery conversations to which we were once privy were few and far between. Dawson would be quick to claim to whomever wanted to debate the issue that Spielberg was, without a shadow of a doubt, a visionary filmmaker. It was more than just the tumultuous teenage affairs that swerved Dawson from the path of film; it was also Nikki Green. The new principal's daughter was gifted. Her film project on dysfunctional American families should have won the Boston film festival but did not. She offered clear-cut advice to Dawson on his *Escape from Witch Island* movie "It's way too derivative," and they were firm friends and rivals from that point onwards. Dawson realized that his whole life centered around film and though Nikki was equally enamored of celluloid, she also had a life beyond the camera.

Dawson paused. He took up photography, took down his Spielberg posters and stopped framing everything in his vision as if for a perfect denouement shot. This was the respite he needed to enable him to pick up the camera with renewed vigour. Arthur Brooks, a gifted filmmaker who had also had his heart broken, allowed Dawson to return to his love with eyes no longer short-sighted from looking at everything from behind a lens. And his first effort, Brooks' documentary, was excellent. But as ever, Dawson is the highly-strung type who spiralled into despair the moment Ms Watson advised him to rewrite his "Why Do You Want To Be A Filmmaker?" essay: "Right this very moment, thousands of students like yourself are composing their essays, pouring their hearts onto paper, hoping against hope for a chance to study at one of the best film schools in the country." It is Gretchen who reminds him of his love, his need for film, which she compares to a girl: "I watched you the other night. Talking about Brooks' movie. And you came alive in a way I had never seen before. You love this girl, Dawson." (Episode #409, *Kiss, Kiss, Bang, Bang.*)

Dawson's application is not enough to gain entry to New York University, though, and the former doubts about his worthiness arise once more: "If NYU doesn't want me, USC is definitely not gonna want me, and where does that leave me?" Gretchen tries to calm him once again, but it is only when Dawson gains entry to the University of Southern California, that he is truly content. Ever since we saw Dawson improvise with a wheelchair to create a smooth tracking shot in *Helmets of Glory* (Cliff Elliot's showboat jock movie way back in Season I), we knew he had what it took to pursue his dream. When Dawson eventually bumps heads with like-minded teens at university, he will realize the drive and determination he had to achieve his dream is widely held by others as well.

WHY DON'T YOU TELL ME WHAT YOU THINK?
We always knew our gang were very advanced for their ages, but surely counseling was something none of them would need until they were at least in their mid-twenties?

Mr Kasdan catches a tipsy Jen during the senior trip, throwing away some liquor bottles. He makes Jen go to counselling sessions with a decidedly cool character, Mr Frost. At first, she is decidedly frosty herself: "I'm not sure I'm the kind of person who would benefit from therapy. I just might be too self-aware for the likes of you." (Episode #415, *Four Stories*) And that is perhaps our gang's – perhaps even this generation's – problem. Self-awareness does not always come in association with an understanding of behavioral patterns. Everyone these days seems to have a master's degree in retrospection, yet people still make decisions unaware of how they are going to affect their futures.

Frost takes the smartass teen comments in his stride. And in silence. It is the silence that Jen becomes uncomfortable with, feeling she has to fill it – at first with idle chit chat – but then with more poignant details. Though Frost's a tad anal when it comes to his office being prim and proper, he certainly understands that, super-smart though Jen is, she is experiencing problems that she is unable to deal with on her own. Frost's first task is to get her to trust him. Frost is not at all surprised when Jen, with her buddy Jack in tow, follows him to a bookstore and even accepts his invitation to a poetry reading given by his girlfriend. He makes her realize that her need to trust people – men in particular – is something she needs to deal with.

Tom Frost (as Jen looks round his super-smart and tidy office): "I apologise for the mess." *Jen:* "You're really quite the slob."

Though Jen is reluctant, her surrogate brother Jack is there to encourage her continued attendance at the sessions: "Now be a good psychologically damaged child and go back to therapy and work this out." What Jen needs to work out is why she is prone to certain self-destructive behaviour patterns. Jen realizes

that if it were not for the love of Grams and her friends in Capeside, she would perhaps be in a worse situation that when she was banished from New York. What Jack is requesting is that Jen resolve the whole father-daughter conflict thing she is working overtime on. Jen's recent resolution with her mother means that she has a better understanding of how callous her father is. Her mother, Helen, desires to leave him but is trapped within the loveless marriage. All Jen can do is pity the fact her mother does not have the strength she does.

Frost bolsters Jen's flagging confidence by assuring her that she needs to resolve her past issues before successfully moving onto the next stage of her life. Jen, self-aware though she may be, resists at first. Frost responds: "When you act out at the age that you did, when you have sex in your parents' bed at 12 years old, when you abuse liquor and drugs before you're even old enough to drive – yes you are doing it as a cry for love... but the reason you keep acting out, the reason you've stayed on a self-destructive path is not because you blame your father... it's because you blame yourself..." (Episode #417, *Admissions*).

Jen confronts her father and the repressed memories about his infidelity are revealed. More importantly, though hurtfully, is that as Jen descended into a spiral of drink, drugs and sex, father observed, knowing he was to blame for her behaviour. Instead of dealing with his daughter's problems, he simply banished them – and her. It's doubtful Mr Lindley ever thought Jen would confront him, but she does. Jen draws the counseling to a close, feeling she has accomplished much. She has worked her way toward believing the beautiful sentiment Frost expressed: "Jennifer, you are a beautiful, innocent young woman who is meant to shine in this world..."

IS THIS YOUR FIRST TIME HERE?

Perhaps the best sexual advice that teens could hear is that unless you are prepared to talk sensibly about sex, you are no where near ready to do it.

It is ironic that Jen's sexual experience means that she is more than qualified to advise the others when they contemplate the er... sticky subject. Cast your minds way back to the second ever episode of *Dawson's Creek*. Joey was working overtime on a jealousy thing going on with Jen, the big boobed newcomer from New York. It was on their way to the Regal theatre – an ill-fated double date with Dawson, Joey, Pacey, and Jen in attendance – when Joey asked: "So, Jen, are you a virgin?... Because Dawson is a virgin and two virgins really makes for a clumsy first encounter, don't you think?" Jen pretends not to notice the electricity in the air and responds: "Yes. I'm a virgin. How about you Joey, are you?" Joey, in white lie mode says she is not a virgin. The initial rules for the war between Jen and Joey over Dawson had been laid.

Skip forward a few years and it is ironic that Joey is given sex advice by Jen. And the man in question is not Dawson but Pacey. Who would have thought it? Joey and Jen have become, if not the best of friends, at least young adults who can talk intelligently to one another about serious issues. Joey expresses her problems: "Of course I wanna have sex, but the question is — am I ready?" Jen's advice is sound. She knows that Joey has the whole emotional thing under wraps and her counsel is centered on the practical: "If you guys are headed toward some sort of sexual culmination, you need to be prepared ahead of time. For girls in New York, a visit to the free clinic to get birth control and safe sex advice is a rite of passage, like a bar mitzvah or a learner's permit test."

Joey did as instructed and was more than a little embarrassed at the free clinic. There would have been teens around the world who squirmed in unison as Joey was hypnotised by some hard facts. The sex counselor trawled though the concerns anyone who is considering a sexual relationship – especially their first one – has to contemplate. The wise counselor reminds Joey to think of the uncomfortable but possible consequences: sexually transmitted diseases such as HIV, chlamydia, syphilis, herpes, and of course, unwanted pregnancy. Just as Joey's embarrassment reaches gargantuan proportions, the counselor takes pause. She reminds Joey of the "wonderful, fun, fulfilling" side to sex and assures her it is "one of the most natural things in the world, something we all have in common." This scene is bound to have helped countless teens who were in a quandary, looking for honest, impartial yet practical advice on their own sexual health. Many teens may have not known where to go for such advice. Seeing Joey, a young feminist heroine, visit such a place would have been an educational moment in itself. Joey, you go, girl!

When Bessie discovers Joey's free bag of gifts – condoms, spermicide, and other forms of birth control – she expresses, in her usual loud manner, her displeasure at the thought of her little sis having sex. Bessie calms down though when her boyfriend Bodie reminds her of the responsible way Joey has approached the issue (Episode #405, A Family Way).

When Joey finally consummates her relationship with Pacey while on the senior ski trip,

Pacey to Joey (During a make out session): "Calm your hormones woman! Didn't anyone ever tell you 'no' means 'no'?"

it is beautiful. They are young teens, truly in love who have expressed themselves physically – and carefully. Though the contraceptive side was well taken care of, who would have thought there would have been all that morning-after emotional fallout? Joey and Pacey can barely look at each other, let alone touch, and Pacey appears to feel it more keenly than Joey. His pride is hurt and in a touching moment, Joey articulates her feelings carefully: "Years from now, when I think back, I'm not gonna remember the clumsy positioning or the morning-after awkwardness, or if the experience itself met the textbook definition of great sex. What I'm gonna remember is how sweet you were… I'm glad I had sex, Pacey. And I'm glad I had sex with you." (Episode #415, *Four Stories*.)

This scene was especially eye-opening as the more sexually experienced Pacey tends to be more comfortable with his sexual needs and desires. His experience with Tamara Jacobs, his former English teacher, means that he can deal with the emotional fallout of a sexual relationship a little better than some others in the gang. Pacey's ex-girlfriend Andie had to learn the hard way that sexual infidelity is extremely hard, if nigh impossible, to forgive. Andie's affair with Marc, while recuperating from her mental illness, was too much for Pacey following their long separation. It is a testament to both teens that they were able to work through that issue and remain, if not together, at least firm friends.

Gretchen to Joey:

"I know that everything seems confusing and frightening, but you have to find the courage to take the test. Then you can consider all your options."

Joey's pregnancy scare made her realize that although she did not want to get pregnant, she could at least face the reality of the situation. Once she had confided to Bessie and apologized for insulting her about her lifestyle, Joey could face taking the pregnancy test. That was a test Joey was glad to fail. It was Gretchen, who had been through a similar experience, who offered the advice Joey needed. It was an ironic situation as Gretchen found herself unable to sleep with Dawson – though he was far from unwilling.

Dawson's battle to lose his virginity took on new dimensions once Joey fell in love with Pacey. Up until the discovery, Dawson still held on dearly to this deliciously romantic vision that he and Joey would lose their virginity together (look at the poignancy Joey's line about two virgins battling it out now takes on). Dawson found it impossibly difficult to deal with Joey and Pacey's relationship. When he discovered there was something going on between the two of them, his eyes were as wide as a Spielberg character who has seen the shark, or the alien, or the dinosaur for the first time.

In fact, Dawson finds it so difficult to contemplate Joey with a young man (besides himself that is), that he actually has the nerve to ask Joey whether she and Pacey are doing it. If Dawson and Joey were merely good friends and did not share an incredibly complex history, the question would have been fine. In fact, it probably would have been a question that need not have been asked, as Joey would have confided – to her buddy Dawson anyway – how happy she was.

But Dawson and Joey are not buddies in that sense. Joey's unrequited feelings for Dawson bubbled and frothed like the creek during a storm. She suffered Dawson's relationship with Jen; then Dawson and Joey finally got it together; then Dawson had to suffer Joey's infidelity (a kiss is still infidelity to these guys) and the subsequent relationship with Jack; then Jack came out as gay and that was a whole new story. When Dawson and Joey got back together, it should have been their time – but it wasn't. Various trials split them asunder. Though Joey once threw herself at Dawson (Episode #301, *Like A Virgin*) it was not meant to be. Hurt and instantly regretful, Joey spat: "It's not my fault if you're still a virgin," but Dawson maintained his dignity – and of course, Joey's.

For all Eve's pawing, Dawson never had sex with her due to circumstances beyond both of their control. There were times when Dawson seemed a little afraid of Eve's blatant sexuality. Though there were definitely teenage boys around the world who groaned at his inability to take opportunities offered to him, they should also acknowledge that it would have been completely out of Dawson's character to do so.

What was not outside of his character though, was Gretchen. A smarter, older woman on whom he had once had a painful crush for years suddenly turned up in town and captivated his heart. She was experienced. He was eager. So why didn't Dawson and Gretchen get it together? Dawson's a smart lad. He must have been – like Joey's experiment while on the senior trip – ever ready with a condom in his wallet. And more importantly to Dawson, he and Gretchen were completely in love. He himself would have never thought it possible that he could grow to love someone as deeply as he did Joey, but he did.

Now, Dawson is not a young man to shy away from uncomfortable situations. He showed that he was a teen responsible enough to discuss sex in an adult manner and eventually worked his way around to questioning Gretchen. While they were on the beach, the time was right for the pair to consummate their relationship – but they didn't: "I really thought you wanted to sleep with me," he says. Gretchen says that it would have been a mistake to get closer to Dawson knowing that they will have to part ways soon. And thus, when they do eventually go their separate ways, Dawson is still a virgin, though definitely not, as he originally and innocently asked Eve at the opening of season III: "What comes before virgin?"

And now we come to a defining moment. The close of Season IV and Dawson and Joey's kiss. Episode #423, *Coda* is an episode that had *Dawson's Creek* bulletin boards blow up even more than usual. Pacey and Joey had broken up, with Pacey leaving Capeside for the summer to cruise in a boat again – but this time not with a young woman who had stolen his heart. Dawson of course, had split from Gretchen as she realized the long-distance relationship thing would not work and that she needed to return to university to finish her studies.

Dawson and Joey's kiss is a tender parting between friends – and actually transcends the issue of sex, although of course, Dawson and Joey discuss it. Says Dawson: "It just hit me… everyone's had sex but me. I never had sex in high school. I was totally planning on doing that. What happened?"

Joey is cognizant of the fact that her relationship with Pacey has changed her. She is able to reflect upon her time with Pacey without denigrating it – as folk are sometimes wont to do in self-defense once a relationship has broken up. Joey acknowledged to Dawson that the magic she shared with Pacey had simply… fizzled out. The kiss with Dawson symbolized their acceptance that they still possessed magic – regardless of what they had been through. These two friends had been through the mill and emerged, if not unscathed, at least intact. Dawson had told Joey not to underestimate him and the things he could deal with, and Joey had ceased being ultra-sensitive about everything. She says it herself, that things had been like a soap opera, but she wouldn't change any of it. The kiss signified a stamp of approval on friendship… and perhaps in the future, more.

The Gang at a Glance

*Are you new to **Dawson's Creek**? Or perhaps you need to brush up on your knowledge of the main players? This quick guide will bring you up to speed on Creek character foibles, some of their best lines and triumphant moments. No reason to feel left out of a **Dawson's Creek** conversation ever again.*

DAWSON LEERY

Nickname	It has been a while, but **Oompa Loompa** is still very likely to get you slammed in the face with a basketball as in Episode #106, *Detention*.
Parents	The on-again, off-again, on-again couple of the millennium, **Mitch** and **Gale**.
Siblings	Finally, Dawson's only-child status has been delightfully wrecked by gorgeous baby sister **Lillian**.
Boyfriend/Girlfriend	It was **Jen**, then **Joey**, then kinda, sorta **Eve**, then **Gretchen** – now he's young, free, single and off to college.
Best Pal	Through all the trials and tribulations, it's still **Joey**.
Most embarrassing moment	Running up to Joey for a hug after almost killing Pacey during the Capeside Regatta and having her ignore him, Episode #321, *Show Me Love*.

Most triumphant moment	Beginning to accept Joey and Pacey's relationship and unclenching enough to realize he cannot control the affections of anyone but himself.
Worst character trait	He talks and talks and talks and talks and talks and talks and talks and talks and talks and talks …
Best character trait	His honesty ability to speak from the heart.
Least likely to say	"I suppose I have taken too long to declare my feelings to Joey, it's OK, Pace, here's wishing you all the best."
Most likely to say	"I've taken down the Spielberg posters in my room. Everything's in question lately." Episode #312, A Weekend in the Country.
Key to understanding	Dawson Leery is unlike any teenage boy you know. His heart is not worn on his sleeve but on his forehead, surrounded by neon flashing lights. He is introspective to the point of inactivity but delightfully honest. Dawson's finally worked through all the angst a teen can handle, and is ready to start deconstructing his college years!

JOSEPHINE POTTER

Nickname	Everyone calls her **Joey** but the way Pacey called her "**Potter**" took on a whole different interpretation recently.
Parents	Her father's still in jail, but it was a delight to see Joey receive a letter from her deceased mother congratulating her on graduating high school, Episode #422 *The Graduate*.
Siblings	The indomitable **Bessie**.
Boyfriend/Girlfriend	It was **Dawson**, then it was **Jack**, then it was **Dawson**, then it was **A.J.** then it was **Pacey**.
Best Pal	Through all the trials and tribulations, it's still **Dawson**.
Most embarrassing moment	Offering herself to Dawson in the midst of his stripper party and have him decline the invitation, Episode #301 *Like A Virgin*.
Most triumphant moment	After nightmares and financial woes, Joey finally gained entry to the university of her dreams, Worthington.
Worst character trait	Not enjoying the moment. Constantly, she would in the midst of happiness with Pacey, refer to Dawson. It was only while at sea for the summer that Dawson was not constantly on her mind, but unfortunately, we never saw her that summer!
Best character trait	Her drive and determination – like Gloria Gaynor says, Joey will survive.
Least likely to say	"I need another bottle of hair colour, in beach blonde ho-bag shade."
Most likely to say	"I'm not looking for surprises today. Just good times and old friends." Episode #422 *The Graduate*.
Key to understanding	Joey is a picture of contradictions. Though she is determined, she is still unsure of herself, unsure of what she wants to do and unsure of her future. It seems as if everybody but Joey can see her potential.

PACEY WITTER

Nickname	**Pace**
Parents	His father **John** is Capeside's unlikely chief of police. We saw his mother **Mary** for the first time in Episode #412, *The Te of Pacey*.
Siblings	Deputy **Doug**, **Gretchen** and at long last, we see **Kerry** (mother of the "no-necked monsters").
Boyfriend/Girlfriend	There was teacher **Tamara Jacobs**, then **Andie**, then a failed attempt at romance with **Jen** and finally **Joey**.
Best Pal	Though his best buddy status with **Dawson** was questioned, they may return to sharing girl anecdotes in time.
Most embarrassing moment	How about having to leave graduation practice in front of all of his friends? Mortifying. Episode #422, *The Graduate*.
Most triumphant moment	Kissing Joey. He followed his gut instinct and it proved to be correct.
Worst character trait	Failing to live up to his educational potential – the rigour and constricting nature of school drives him mad.
Best character trait	His wit and charm could make birds fly down from the sky.
Least likely to say	"Give me a minute, I'm thinking, I'm thinking."
Most likely to say	"Even if that means waiting forever." Episode #414, *A Winter's Tale*.
Key to understanding	Pacey is messed up but honest and the kind of friend who will always, always watch your back. A guy's guy.

JENNIFER LINDLEY

Nickname	**Jen**
Parents	**Helen**, unhappy with her husband, the insidious **Theodore**, bane of Jen's young life.
Siblings	None
Boyfriend/Girlfriend	**Dawson** then **Cliff**, then **Ty**, then **Henry**, now single!
Best Pal	**Jack** is more of a surrogate brother than a friend.
Most embarrassing moment	Accidentally letting slip to Dawson that Pacey and Joey are seeing each other Episode #320, *The Longest Day*.
Most triumphant moment	Learning to trust her counsellor Tom Frost to enable her sessions to be more beneficial.
Worst character trait	Her "glass-half-empty" attitude. It took poor Henry Parker an age to convince her of the veracity of his intentions.
Best character trait	Her ability to learn from her mistakes.
Least likely to say	"Have you got any other arts and crafts you'd like to teach me Grams?"
Most likely to say	"I have issues." Episode #319, *Stolen Kisses*.
Key to understanding	Jen's counseling sessions revealed much to us about her past. She is a lot more complex than we had given her credit for and her determination to overcome her problems is admirable. A girl's girl.

JACK MCPHEE

Nickname	**Jackers**
Parents	His mother **Betsy** is unwell, following a nervous breakdown and his dad **Joseph** has only recently returned to Capeside.
Siblings	There's **Andie** and surrogate sister **Jen**. His elder brother **Tim** died in a car crash.
Boyfriend/Girlfriend	There was **Kate**, then **Joey** then a failed attempt at his first gay relationship with **Ethan** before finding happiness with **Tobey**.
Best Pal	**Jen**
Most embarrassing moment	Kissing Ethan in front of his boyfriend after a long road trip. Painful. Episode #323, *True Love*.
Most triumphant moment	Finally, after starting out claiming to hate the the guy, Jack admits his true feelings for Tobey and kisses him, Episode #420, *Promicide*.
Worst character trait	His procrastination. He will put off thinking about his emotions when people around him have already figured things out for him!
Best character trait	His devotion to his sister Andie and best friend Jen.
Least likely to say	"Let's get this party started right."
Most likely to say	While failing to emulate Grams' skill in home arts and crafts: "It's moments like these where I'm convinced I'm straight." Episode #321, *Show Me Love*.
Key to understanding	Perhaps the shyest character, Jack has definitely grown more confident recently. While his homosexuality helps to define Jack it is not his defining feature. He is great at applications, succeeded at football, and helps friends challenge themselves.

ANDIE McPHEE

Nickname	Her grade school nickname was **Andie McGeek**
Parents	**Betsy** and **Joseph**
Siblings	**Jack**. It was her brother **Tim's** death that contributed to her mental illness.
Boyfriend/Girlfriend	It was **Pacey**, then infidelity with **Marc**, then a few dates with **Rob Logan**, then **Will**, then a fun time with **J.J.**
Best Pal	Andie is friends with everyone – and does not really have a best, best pal.
Most embarrassing moment	Taking Ecstasy – not a smart thing for a smart girl to do, especially when they're on anti–depressants, Episode #406, *Great Xpectations*.
Most triumphant moment	Impressing the socks off a bewildered Mrs Valentine, Episode #403, *Two Gentlemen of Capeside*.
Worst character trait	Her insistence at being the best at everything – school, college applications, recovering from challenging situations.
Best character trait	Her smartness – this girl is gonna go far!
Least likely to say	"This homework is not really important, I'm just going to leave it."
Most likely to say	Overcome by the gang being together during Thanksgiving, Andie reminisces: "I love 'A Charlie Brown Thanksgiving.' That's the one where they have dinner on the ping pong table…" Episode #308, *Guess Who's Coming To Dinner*.
Key to understanding	Andie is a highly strung genius plagued more by her own imagination than real events. But more than anything she is a survivor.

GRETCHEN WITTER

Nickname	None generally used and most of Pacey's are unprintable
Parents	**John** and **Mary**
Siblings	The inimitable **Pacey**, Deputy **Doug**, and **Kerry**
Boyfriend/Girlfriend	We met **Nasty Nick** and were we glad she fell for Dawson or what?
Best Pal	Her pals **Keira** and **Jessica** shock Dawson with their girl talk but that's what friends are for.
Most embarrassing moment	Seeing Dawson walk away from her countless times, perhaps most poignantly during Episode #420, *Promicide*
Most triumphant moment	Realising that despite her love for Dawson, she needed to move on with her life and continue her education. Her beautiful message in his yearbook said it all. Episode #421, *Separation Anxiety*.
Worst character trait	Getting stuck in the middle. Though she's in a relationship with Dawson, she should have striven harder to ensure he didn't always drag Joey into their most intimate moments.
Best character trait	She stuck with Dawson through his traumatic trials. She's faithfully honest about her insecurities and helps others to overcome their own fears.
Least likely to say	"Come on Doug and Pacey, let's go round to Mum and Dad's for dinner."
Most likely to say	"My life is going nowhere..." – Episode #420, *Promicide*, but perhaps not now that she has returned to college.
Key to understanding	Gretchen is a mature girl who went through a difficult period. Though she was reluctant to love Dawson, she couldn't help herself and fell head over heels. This helped her achieve closure with Nick and eventually return to her education. Not a young woman to be trifled with.

DRUE VALENTINE

Nickname	"… **lame TV-Batman villain** …" according to Dawson.
Parents	Mr and Mrs Valentine are estranged and Drue cannot stand either parent.
Siblings	None
Boyfriend/Girlfriend	**Anna Evans** was left in tears after a liaison with Drue, is it any surprise he is terminally single?
Best Pal	Ha! The only person he can rely on in times of need is **Jen** – and even then he has to beg like the mongrel he is, Episode #422, *The Graduate*.
Most embarrassing moment	Getting suspended from school for the stunning senior trick – Principal Peskin's boat in the school swimming pool – especially as he did not do it.
Most triumphant moment	Admitting his problems with women to Joey (but lo and behold an episode later he's back to his usual misogyny).
Worst character trait	Where to start? The drug-peddling, the lying, the cheating, the acid tongue, the constant childish pranks…
Best character trait	His wit – you gotta give him his due, Drue is a funny guy.
Least likely to say	"I take it all back."
Most likely to say	"Ladies and gentleman, I present to you the marveling, idiotic mental feats of Anna Evans. Warning: don't try this at home or with more than two brain cells" (Episode #413, *Hopeless*). And remember, this is how he talks about the woman he is dating!
Key to understanding	There's little to understand – Drue is naturally wicked. Yes he has problems but there are others with worse problems and a less evil disposition. New York has lost one of its truly rotten seeds but unfortunately, it has taken root in Capeside.